Tokyo 2020 Olympics

A Wiley Brand

Tokyo 2020 Olympics

by Celeste Kiyoko Hall

Tokyo 2020 Olympics For Dummies®

Published by: **John Wiley & Sons, Inc.**, 111 River Street, Hoboken, NJ 07030-5774, www.wiley.com

Copyright © 2020 by John Wiley & Sons, Inc., Hoboken, New Jersey

Published simultaneously in Canada

For general information on our other products and services, please contact our Customer Care Department within the U.S. at 877-762-2974, outside the U.S. at 317-572-3993, or fax 317-572-4002. For technical support, please visit https://hub.wiley.com/community/support/dummies.

Wiley publishes in a variety of print and electronic formats and by print-on-demand. Some material included with standard print versions of this book may not be included in e-books or in print-on-demand. If this book refers to media such as a CD or DVD that is not included in the version you purchased, you may download this material at http://booksupport.wiley.com. For more information about Wiley products, visit www.wiley.com.

Library of Congress Control Number: 2019957440

ISBN 978-1-119-66409-3 (ebk); ISBN 978-1-119-66412-3 (ebk); ISBN 978-1-119-66408-6 (ebk)

Manufactured in the United States of America

V10016835_010920

Contents at a Glance

Table of Contents

Introduction

Are you excited to head to Japan for the Tokyo 2020 Summer Olympics? Or maybe you're more than a little intimidated by planning a trip to a foreign country for one of the biggest sporting events in the world? Maybe a little bit of both? Regardless, you've found the right book!

Planning a trip to Japan can be stressful but manageable and even exciting if you've got a game plan. By the end of this book, you should have a solid idea of how to make sure you have everything in order to have a smooth trip.

About This Book

Tokyo 2020 Olympics For Dummies is a Japan travel guidebook and Tokyo 2020 Summer Olympics event guide combined into one. The reality is that some of the normal Japan travel tips and recommendations such as "top ten hotels in Tokyo to stay in" get thrown out the window due to the Olympics. In this book, I tell you everything you need to know specifically for planning a trip to Japan for the Olympics.

The best part is that this book doesn't have to be read in order. If you've already started planning your trip or there are only certain pieces of information you're interested in, feel free to use the Table of Contents and Index to skip around.

Also, all prices listed within the book are current as of this writing and are listed in either the U.S. dollar ($) or the Japanese yen (¥). Any prices listed in yen have the U.S. dollar equivalent in parentheses. I calculated the dollar amount based off the exchange rate at the time of this writing, which was $1 = ¥109.

Throughout this book, I also mention soccer as one of the Olympic sports. Outside of the United States, this sport is known as football.

Finally, within this book, you may note that some web addresses break across two lines of text. If you're reading this book in print and you want to visit one of these web pages, simply key in the web address exactly as it's noted in the text, pretending as though the line break doesn't exist. If you're reading this as an e-book, you've got it easy — just click the web address to be taken directly to the web page.

Foolish Assumptions

We all know what assumptions do, but in order to write this book, I had to make a few anyway:

>> **You're planning to go to Japan for the Summer Olympics.** This book contains useful information if you're going to Japan during another part of the year or you're watching the Olympics at home on your couch. But not all the information will be applicable.

>> **You may or may not have traveled to Japan before.** If you're new to Japan, this book has everything you need to feel confident about your trip. If you've been to Japan before, you may want to skip ahead to Part 2 for Olympics-specific information — but you'll still find useful tips throughout the book!

>> **You can purchase tickets and book accommodations.** Tickets for the Tokyo 2020 Olympic events have been very hard to come by. Accommodations have also been scarce and priced significantly higher than the norm. I guide you through how to buy tickets and book accommodations, but in doing so, I assume that tickets are available for purchase and rooms are available to book — which they may not be.

Icons Used in This Book

To make sure you don't miss important details, we use the following icons throughout this book. Here's what the different icons mean:

TIP

Planning a trip involves a lot of moving parts. Anything marked with the Tip icon highlights specific tips that can make your life easier or call out things that would be easy to miss.

The Remember icon is primarily used to call out specific pieces of information that will be beneficial to remember (or at least jot down somewhere).

Mistakes can not only add additional stress to your trip, but also blow your budget. The Warning icon calls out some of those easy-to-make mistakes you'll want to avoid.

Beyond the Book

In addition to what you're reading right now, this book also comes with a free, access-anywhere Cheat Sheet that provides some of the key pieces of information you'll need to know before your trip, as well as helpful tips. It also includes a high-level overview of the Olympics and Japan as a whole. To view the Cheat Sheet, simply go to www.dummies.com and type **Tokyo 2020 Olympics For Dummies Cheat Sheet** in the Search box.

Olympics-related information is accurate as of this writing. However, unforeseen events may cause the International Olympic Committee to make changes to the Olympic events after the publication of this book. For the most up-to-date information about the Tokyo 2020 Summer Olympics, visit the official website for the Olympic and Paralympic Games Tokyo 2020 at https://tokyo2020.org.

If you're just dying to know more about Japanese culture, history, and tourism, I recommend checking out these resources:

>> **Japan National Tourism Organization (JNTO):** www.jnto.go.jp

>> **Japan Travel and Living Guide:** https://japan-guide.com

>> **A Dreamer Traveling to Japan:** https://footstepsofadreamer.com/category/asia/japan

Where to Go from Here

Part 1 of this book covers the key things you need to make sure you have in order before getting on a plane to Japan. To make your life easier, I recommend starting here.

If you're stressed about the actual planning part of your trip, check out Part 3, which covers getting tickets, reserving accommodations, and booking plane tickets.

Part 4 will help you get oriented after you land in Japan. However, I recommend at least glancing through this section before you go. Knowing what to expect can help reduce some of the culture shock you may experience when you first get to Japan.

Part 2 is specifically about the Tokyo 2020 Summer Olympics, and it'll make a great read on a long flight.

1

Getting Ready to Travel to Tokyo

IN THIS PART . . .

Get familiar with Japan and the Tokyo 2020 Olympics.

Put together necessary travel documents.

Make sure your phone will work in Japan.

Figure out what to pack.

Chapter **1**

Feeling the Olympic Spirit

You're going to the Olympics! Well, at least, you're planning to. It's exciting and scary, thrilling yet intimidating. The idea of taking a trip, exploring someplace new (or rediscovering a place you've already been to), and going on an adventure is amazing! Planning it is often less so. Planning an international trip for one of the biggest sporting events in the world may even seem like a total nightmare, but don't worry. I get you through it. This chapter offers you a mini-preview of what you can find throughout *Tokyo 2020 Olympics For Dummies*.

Taking Care of Business

There are some things you'll need to get done before you go on your trip, such as making sure you have a valid passport. You won't get real far without one. You may also need to speak with your doctor to discuss any recommended vaccinations or what you'll do with any prescription medication you may have (because bringing certain medications to Japan can be a bit complicated). Turn to Chapter 2 for more on all these details.

When you've got all your paperwork in order, the next question that tends to pop into people's minds is, "What am I going to do about my cellphone?" or more accurately, "How am I going to connect to the Internet?" The good news is: A variety of places in Japan, including Starbucks and McDonald's, offer free Wi-Fi. However, for most people, jumping from hotspot to hotspot isn't exactly the most ideal.

In this case, you have a couple of different options: an international phone plan, SIM card, or Wi-Fi pack. Each has its own advantages depending on what kind of traveler you are. International phone plans will be good for those who just don't want to have to deal with the hassle, but will also likely be the most expensive option. If you want something more budget friendly, you'll want to go with a SIM card or portable Wi-Fi pack. If you have multiple devices that you need to have connected to the Internet at any given point in time (such as every person in your family wanting a functioning phone during the trip), go with the Wi-Fi pack. Otherwise, a SIM card will be your best bet. For more information about international phone plans, SIM cards, and Wi-Fi packs, check out Chapter 3.

Next comes the fun part: figuring out what to actually take with you to Japan (see Chapter 4). Depending on what part of the United States you're from, the weather in Japan could be drastically different from what you're used to, or it could be pretty similar.

WARNING

Then, of course, there is always the issue of overpacking. I hate to break it to you but, just because you're going on a 15-day vacation does not mean you need to pack 14 different shirts. Most hotels have laundry facilities for you to be able to wash your clothes. Do yourself a favor and save the space in your luggage for souvenirs and all the other things you'll pick up along the way. If not, you'll find yourself paying not only for a new suitcase to fit all your souvenirs but also additional baggage fees at the airport.

Most important though, just make sure you bring the things you can't replace, like your travel documents, identification, medication, glasses, and other similar items. If you forget your toothbrush, I guarantee you'll be able to find a cheap one at a local convenience store after you land in Japan. The place you're staying may even provide one free of charge.

Knowing What to Expect from the Games

The 2020 Summer Olympics are shaping up to be quite the spectacular event, but there are a lot of moving pieces to it. A total of 33 different sports will be appearing at this Summer Olympics. Over the course of two weeks, there will be more than 700 different events. If that's not a jam-packed schedule, then I don't know what is.

One of the best parts of the Olympics is that sports that normally don't get talked about are suddenly in the limelight. Other than during the previous Summer Olympics, when was the last time you watched an archery competition or table tennis match? Just in case there are a few sports you aren't super familiar with, you can find an introduction to each of the sports in Chapter 6.

An often overlooked part of the Games are the event venues themselves (see Chapter 5). Unfortunately, despite it being the Tokyo Olympics, not all the venues are located in Tokyo. Most of them are at least in the general vicinity, but a few don't exactly make for easy day trips (yes, I'm looking at you, Sapporo Dome — almost *nine hours* from Tokyo by train!). You'll want to make sure to familiarize yourself with the different venue locations before you start buying tickets to make sure you don't have two events back to back without enough time to travel between them.

Also, did you know that more than just sporting events go on during the Olympics? Part of the mission of the International Olympic Committee is to "encourage the regular practice of sport by all people in society, regardless of sex, age, social background, or economic status." To help encourage that, Partner Houses will be set up by representatives of various countries and sports federations, allowing visitors to experience different cultures and sports while meeting new people.

Aside from the Partner Houses, a special festival called the TOKYO 2020 NIPPON FESTIVAL will be held to help build enthusiasm in the Olympics. Various events throughout this festival will help not only promote the Olympic mission of bringing people together but also allow participants to interact with and experience Japanese culture, similar to the way that athletes from all over the world will be interacting with each other during the Games. You can find more information about some of the other Olympics-related events in Chapter 8.

Going into Planning Mode

Honestly, I think planning a trip is almost as fun as actually going on a trip, but I'm just weird like that.

Some people prefer to just go with the wind and sort of figure things out as they go. I highly recommend not doing that, at least for this trip. For the past several Olympics, tickets to events were sometimes available for sale right up to the start of the event.

WARNING

Given the unprecedented ticket demand that has been seen thus far, the chances of tickets being available for purchase right before the events will be slim. You'd hate to make it all the way to Japan and then not be able to get any tickets to any of the events. Get more info on buying tickets in Chapter 9.

The same goes for booking flights and hotels (see Chapter 10). Booking flights last minute is almost always more costly, regardless of where you're going, but sometimes holding off on reserving accommodations can pay off if the hotel has a lot of vacancies. However, this is very, very unlikely to happen during the Olympics. If you haven't already done so, I definitely recommend purchasing tickets for the events, flights, and accommodations sooner rather than later.

The sort of optional last step is simply to create an actual travel itinerary (see Chapter 11). Personally, I like making at least a rough itinerary, because if I don't, my conversations with my travel companions usually turn into something like, "What do you want to do? I don't know, what do you want to do? I don't know." All we end up doing is wasting precious time that we could be using to explore the city or relax in an *onsen* (Japanese hot spring).

However, not everybody likes having a set-in-stone itinerary, and that's okay. Some people find it to be very stressful if they feel like they have to be at a certain place by a certain time, which can take away from the overall enjoyment of the trip. If this sounds like you, no big deal. Just make sure to at least be cognizant of what times you'll need to be at the different venues for the tickets you purchased and approximately how long it will take you to get there.

Getting Around Japan

The first time I went to Japan, I wasn't super nervous about the flight or making sure I had everything in order. No, I was worried about how I would actually *survive* in the country. Would I be able to communicate with others? How did the train system work? Was I accidentally going to offend somebody or insult their culture? Thankfully, it ended up being much easier than I expected.

I recommend at least becoming somewhat familiar with life in Japan before departing on your trip. It will make getting over the culture shock significantly easier. (Chapter 16 can help with this.)

Most important, you'll want to take a look at the currency system. You don't need to have all the different coins and bills memorized, but know that Japan is a very cash-driven society. Unlike the United States where you can use a debit or credit card seemingly everywhere, you'll find that most smaller, mom-and-pop-type shops in Japan won't accept cards. Being prepared for this in advance will help you decide whether you want to order yen at your local bank before you depart and how you'll get cash while in Japan. You can find more info about currency and payment methods in Chapter 13.

I also recommend reading up on the train system (see Chapter 15). It will most likely be your primary mode of transportation while you're in Japan. It's not terribly difficult, but it is extensive, which can be a little overwhelming for first-time visitors. Knowing what to do before you actually get to the train station for the first time will definitely make your life a bit less stressful.

If you don't look up anything else about the train system before your trip, at least look into the Japan Rail Pass, often shortened to just JR Pass. These train passes can potentially save you a significant amount of money on train fares, particularly if you plan on traveling outside Tokyo. They're only available to international visitors and until recently could only be bought outside of Japan through authorized retailers. Now, Japan Rail Passes are available for purchase in select train stations, but they're significantly more expensive than if you were to buy them before arriving in Japan.

If you plan to order a Japan Rail Pass before your trip, know that it typically takes about two business days for it to arrive, so make sure you order it at least a week or so before you depart (but preferably much sooner than that).

The other question I often get from people planning to travel to Japan for the first time is, "Will I need to know any Japanese?" My answer is typically no, but with an asterisk attached.

In general, the bigger the city you're in, the more likely you are to find people who speak decent English. Also, younger people and businessmen will likely speak better English than people who don't work outside the home. Granted, those are very blanket statements and will definitely not hold true 100 percent of the time.

Some people move to Japan and live there for several years and never learn a single word of Japanese. Obviously that's a pretty extreme case, but it is possible. However, I also went to some places in downtown Tokyo where none of the staff spoke English and I had to use Japanese if I wanted to be able to communicate with them.

In my opinion, if you never learn a single word of Japanese, you'll probably be just fine. However, learning at least a few basic words (see Chapter 14) can make your trip significantly less stressful.

Making the Most of Your Time in Japan

Last but not least, I recommend taking advantage of your time in Japan to not only attend the Olympic Games, but also to explore Japan. Chances are, you'll inadvertently explore Tokyo (see Chapter 11) as you make your way to all the different venues for the events, but there is so much more to Japan than just Tokyo.

Depending on how much time you have and what your budget is, you may only be able to take one day trip from Tokyo (see Chapter 17), but do it if you can. Many amazing places are just outside of Tokyo, and they may allow you to experience a whole other side of Japan, despite the fact that you only went an hour or so out of the city.

The best part is that there are day trips for every type of traveler. If you're more of an outdoors person, you can head to the Fuji Five Lakes or maybe even climb Mount Fuji. If you'd rather just sit back and relax, you can take a getaway to Hakone and relax in their various hot springs. History buffs and lovers of Japanese culture will want to look toward Nikko or Kamakura or both. Those looking for more off-the-beaten-path destinations can venture up north to Sendai, or out west to Nagoya, both of which have their own unique features.

However, if you have the flexibility, I highly recommend taking more than just a day trip (see Chapter 18). I lived in Tokyo, so it will always hold a special place in my heart, but I'd be hard pressed to say that it was my favorite city in all Japan.

If you don't go anywhere else, go to Hiroshima. Honestly, it's not typically at the top of most people's Japan bucket list, but its historical significance definitely makes it worth visiting and is typically why I recommend it so highly. Learning about World War II and the atomic bomb in school is one thing. Actually visiting Hiroshima and seeing all the memorials is a whole other level.

The other city that comes in at the top of my recommendations list is Kyoto. Unlike Tokyo, which boasts Japan's modernization and technological advancements, Kyoto seems to be a city frozen in history. It's full of sites rich in culture and history, making it a fantastic place to really take a deep dive into traditional Japanese culture.

Of course, Hiroshima and Kyoto aren't the only two worthwhile cities. Japan is full of amazing destinations all across the country (many of which are conveniently located between Tokyo and Hiroshima). I cover a handful of them, but I also recommend doing some of your own research to see what catches your eye.

IN THIS CHAPTER

» Getting a new passport or renewing an existing one

» Making sure you have the appropriate vaccines

» Determining which of your medications you can bring with you

» Discovering different options for travel insurance

» Making sure you have everything you need to enter Japan

Chapter **2**
Taking Care of the Details

You need to have a few really important things in order if you want to visit Japan for the Olympics. Without them, you'll either not even be able to get into the country or run the risk of potentially having a really rough time in Japan. In order to make sure you have a smooth trip, you'll want to get these things done first.

Obtaining a Passport

If you've never gotten a passport before, don't worry. It's not a hard process. It just takes a bit of time to complete. If you need to get a new passport, check out the following sections to find everything you need to know in order to get your U.S. passport.

TIP

If you aren't a U.S. citizen, you'll need to check with the passport agency of your country of citizenship to find the requirements. Here are the websites for the passport agencies of several predominantly English-speaking countries (if your country of citizenship isn't on this list, just search the web for "*country passport*," where *country* is the name of your country):

>> **Australia:** www.passports.gov.au

>> **Canada:** www.canada.ca/en/immigration-refugees-citizenship/services/canadian-passports.html

>> **Ireland:** www.dfa.ie/passports

>> **New Zealand:** www.passports.govt.nz

>> **United Kingdom:** www.gov.uk/browse/abroad/passports

If you already have a U.S. passport but it has either already expired or will expire within six months of returning home from Japan, check out the "Renewing Your Passport" section, later in this chapter, to see if you meet the requirements to renew your passport.

Deciding between types of passports

There are actually two types of U.S. passports: the U.S. passport book and the U.S. passport card. Both can serve as proof of both your U.S. citizenship and identity. However, they have different uses, so it's important that you pick the correct one.

TIP

If you plan to travel to Japan from the United States, you need a valid U.S. passport book.

WARNING

The U.S. passport card is valid for domestic air travel as well as entry into the United States by land or by sea from Canada, Mexico, the Caribbean, or Bermuda. It cannot be used for international air travel. The passport card was designed specifically for people who cross the border by land on a regular basis (such as those who live near the U.S.–Canada or U.S.–Mexico border).

REMEMBER

When filling out the paperwork for a new passport, you'll have the option to select U.S. Passport Book, U.S. Passport Card, or Both. If you plan on frequently traveling to Canada, Mexico, the Caribbean, or Bermuda by land or by sea in the future, feel free to select the Both option (although be aware it will be more expensive). Otherwise, make sure to select the U.S. Passport Book option.

Pulling together everything you need to get a passport

The first thing you need to do is complete Form DS-11. Don't be intimidated by the numbers and letters — it's just the fancy government labeling for the Application for a U.S. Passport form.

This form is available on the U.S. Department of State's website. You can either fill out the form online through the Form Filler system (https://pptform.state.gov) or print out a PDF version of the form (https://eforms.state.gov/Forms/ds11.pdf) and fill it out by hand. Regardless of which option you choose, you need to print out the form and submit it in person at one of the accepted locations (more on accepted locations in the next section).

In additional to a completed Form DS-11, you'll also need to provide proof of U.S. citizenship. For most people, providing a certified birth certificate will be the best option. If you're a U.S. citizen but you were born outside of the United States, you can provide a Report of Birth Abroad, a Certificate of Naturalization, or a Certificate of Citizenship.

You must also provide identification. Technically, this is different from providing proof of citizenship, but in many cases the documents that prove citizenship also provide photo identification. Valid forms of photo identification include the following:

>> In-state, valid driver's license (If you have an out-of-state driver's license, you have to provide a second form of identification, such as Social Security card, voter registration card, or student ID, in addition to your driver's license.)

>> Government employee ID

>> Military ID

>> Current and valid foreign passport

>> U.S. Permanent Resident Card (Green Card)

>> Trusted Traveler ID (Global Entry, for example)

>> Certificate of Naturalization

>> Certificate of Citizenship

Note that you'll also be asked to provide a photocopy of both your proof of citizenship and identification. The photocopies will be kept by the U.S. Department of State for their records. Photocopies must be in black and white and on standard 8.5-x-11-inch printing paper. They must also be single sided. This means that if you're providing your driver's license as identification, the scan of both the front and back of your license needs to be on the same side of the paper.

Finally, you'll be asked to provide a photograph that is to be used for the passport. However, it can't be just any photo. The U.S. Department of State has strict policies when it comes to what's considered an acceptable photo:

>> The photo must be in color (not black and white).

>> The photo must be free of enhancements or filters.

>> The photo must have a plain white or off-white background.

>> The photo must be 2 x 2 inches in size, and the head (from the bottom of the chin to the top of the head) must be 1 inch to 1⅜ inches in length.

>> The photo must be printed on matte or glossy photo-quality paper.

>> The photo may not be damaged or have creases or smudges.

>> The photo cannot be a selfie (it should be taken by somebody else or with a timer).

>> You may not wear glasses or any other accessories that would obstruct your face, such as a hat or head covering. If you wear a head covering for religious or medical purposes, you'll need to submit a signed statement, and your face must still be fully visible.

>> You must have a neutral facial expression or a natural smile, with both eyes open.

>> You must be directly facing the camera so that your full face is in view.

>> You must wear clothing you wear on a normal basis. No uniforms (or clothing that looks like a uniform) or camouflage.

Examples of acceptable photos can be found on the U.S. Department of State's website at https://travel.state.gov/content/travel/en/passports/how-apply/photos.html.

TIP

Your best bet is probably to go to a location where you live and pay to have a passport photo taken. Many Walgreens and CVS drugstores take passport photos, as do many UPS Stores. If you're not sure what's available in your area, search the web for "passport photos near me" or "passport photos *city state*" (where *city* and *state* are the names of the city and state where you live).

WARNING

Be aware that passports for children under 16 may require additional paperwork and steps to be completed (especially if the parents are separated). More information about applying for passports for minors can be found on the government information and services website, USAGov (www.usa.gov/passport-item-212655).

Of course, you'll also have to pay for your passport, so you may want to make sure you have funds prepared as well. Application fees vary based on whether you're applying for an adult or child passport, as well as whether you chose to apply strictly for a passport book or both the passport book and card. As of this writing, the fees are as follows:

>> **Adult passport book:** $110

>> **Adult passport book and card:** $140

>> **Child passport book:** $80

>> **Child passport book and card:** $95

Also note that there is an additional $35 execution or acceptance fee, regardless of the type of passport you're applying for. For example, if you apply for an adult passport book, your total cost would be $145 ($110 adult passport book + $35 execution fee), assuming you don't choose expedited processing or delivery (more on this in the next sections).

Applying for a passport in plenty of time

You must apply for your passport in person. At this point in time, you aren't able to mail in your application or submit it online. Where you should submit your paperwork will depend on how quickly you need your passport.

If your trip is less than three weeks away, you need to visit a passport agency or center in person. In this case, you also need to bring proof of travel (such as a flight itinerary, hotel reservation, or itinerary from a travel agency). Those who expedite their passport applications at a passport agency typically receive their passports in eight business days.

Note that you must schedule an appointment in order to be able to visit, and the appointment must occur within two weeks of your trip. For example, if today is July 1, 2020, and your flight is on July 23, 2020, you'll only be able to schedule your appointment for July 9 or later. Appointments can be scheduled online through the U.S. Department of State's Online Passport Appointment System (https://passportappointment.travel.state.gov).

If your trip is more than three weeks away, you should apply through one of the passport acceptance facilities. You can use the U.S. Department of State's website to locate an acceptance facility near you (https://iafdb.travel.state.gov).

If your trip is less than eight weeks away, the U.S. Department of State recommends selecting the expedited option at the acceptance facility when you submit your paperwork, which will cost an additional $60. In order to get your passport even faster, you can also choose the one- or two-day delivery option for an additional $16.48 fee.

Those who expedite their passport applications at one of the acceptance facilities typically receive their passports in two to three weeks. Those who choose the routine (non-expedited) option typically receive them in six to eight weeks.

Renewing Your Passport

If you already have a U.S. passport but it has expired or will expire within six months of returning home from Japan, you may be able to renew your passport instead of having to get a new one.

If you're a citizen of a country other than the United States, check with your country's passport agency for the renewal requirements.

Determining whether you need to renew your passport

Many countries require that your passport be valid for at least six months past your intended return date. This means that if you intend to return home on August 10, 2020, your passport must be valid until at least February 10, 2021.

TIP

The good news: Japan is not one of these countries. Japan only requires that your passport be valid through the intended time of stay in Japan.

However, if your passport expiration date is close to your return date, I recommend going ahead and renewing your passport anyway. Passports are good for ten years (assuming you're over 16 years old), so renewing a couple of months before the expiration date won't make a big difference and may save you some headaches down the road if you end up being in Japan longer than expected.

Determining whether you can renew your passport

There are very specific situations in which you can renew your passport. You must be able to answer "yes" to all the following questions:

>> Do you have your current passport in your possession and are you physically able to submit it with your renewal application?

>> Is your current passport in good condition (not damaged beyond normal wear and tear)?

>> Was your current passport issued to you when you were 16 years old or older?

>> Was your current passport issued within the last 15 years? (It can't have been expired for 5 years or more.)

>> Does your current passport have your current name, or can you document your name change?

If you answer "no" to any of these questions, you must apply for a new passport (see the previous section, "Obtaining a Passport").

Getting the Required Vaccinations

The Centers for Disease Control (CDC) recommends that travelers be up to date on all routine vaccines before traveling to Japan. Examples of routine vaccines would be the measles, mumps, and rubella (MMR) vaccine and the chicken pox vaccine.

Additional vaccines may be recommended depending on what activities you plan to do and which areas of Japan you plan to visit.

TIP

In all cases, consult with your doctor to ensure you receive any necessary vaccines before your trip. More information about recommended vaccines can be found on the CDC website at https://wwwnc.cdc.gov/travel/destinations/traveler/none/japan.

Bringing Your Medications

Japan has somewhat strict rules when it comes to bringing medications into the country. In general, you can bring up to a two months' supply of over-the-counter medication and up to a one month's supply of prescription medication. However, there are several exceptions to this rule.

The first thing to note is that over-the-counter medications that have stimulants that make up more than 10 percent of the ingredients are forbidden. You'll mostly see this with some allergy, sinus, and cold medications that are available in the United States. For example, Sudafed, a common decongestant, contains pseudoephedrine, which is considered a stimulant and is, therefore, forbidden.

Stimulant drugs such as heroin, cocaine, opium, and marijuana are strictly forbidden, even if they were obtained legally. You read that correctly. You cannot bring marijuana with you to Japan even if it was prescribed to you by a doctor. Other stimulants such as methamphetamines and amphetamines are also prohibited even if you have a prescription. These tend to occur in attention deficit/hyperactivity disorder (ADHD) and sleep disorder medications.

Other types of prescription medications (such as narcotics), as well as medications where you need more than one month's supply, will require a special permit called a *Yakkan Shoumei* (www.us.emb-japan.go.jp/english/html/medication-info-japan.html). Applications for a Yakkan Shoumei should be submitted to one of the Narcotics Controls Departments (NCDs) in Japan at least two weeks in advance.

These regulations may change at any time, so check the Japan Ministry of Health, Labour, and Welfare website at www.mhlw.go.jp/english/policy/health-medical/pharmaceuticals/01.html before your trip to ensure you have the most up-to-date information.

For more specifics regarding medication restrictions, you can contact the Japan Ministry of Health, Labour, and Welfare by phone or email. Contact information is available on the website.

Buying Travel and Medical Insurance

When it comes to travel, many people wonder whether they should buy insurance. However, before I can answer that question, I first need to go over the two types of insurance: travel insurance and travel medical insurance. Yes, there is a difference (but most insurance options include both).

Standard travel insurance covers the financial investments of trips such as lost luggage, travel delays, and canceled trips in certain situations (such as illness, a death in the family, or a natural disaster).

Standard travel medical insurance covers healthcare costs incurred while out of the country (for example, if you end up having to visit the hospital or need emergency medical evacuation).

If you were going on a last-minute or cheap domestic flight, I'd tell you to pass on the travel insurance, because you don't have a ton of money at risk and your normal health insurance plan should cover any potential medical emergencies. However, for a trip to Japan, where you've invested a significant amount of money and your normal health insurance won't cover you, I definitely recommend getting travel insurance. Getting travel insurance will ensure that you don't lose out on the thousands of dollars you likely spent on plane tickets, hotel accommodations, and Olympic event tickets.

Many travelers turn to World Nomads (www.worldnomads.com/usa) or Allianz Travel (www.allianztravelinsurance.com) for insurance, as their policies offer both traditional travel insurance, as well as medical insurance. Also, check with your credit card provider. Many travel credit cards offer travel insurance and travel medical insurance as additional benefits.

Understanding Japanese Entry Requirements

The good news is that if you're a U.S. citizen and will be in Japan for less than 90 days (which you most likely will be), you won't need a visa. Just be aware that all visitors entering visa-free will be fingerprinted and photographed upon arrival. More information on this can be found on the Embassy of Japan in the United States of America website (www.us.emb-japan.go.jp/itpr_en/travel_and_visa.html).

If you're not a U.S. citizen, you can check the Ministry of Foreign Affairs of Japan website (www.mofa.go.jp/j_info/visit/visa/index.html) to determine whether you need a visa.

In order to enter the country, you need at least one blank page in your passport for the entry stamp and you must have proof of onward travel (proof that you'll be leaving Japan), such as a booked flight.

Also, be aware that Japanese immigration officers have the right to deny you entry if you appear to have no visible means of support (no credit cards, debit cards, cash, or other means of supporting yourself financially), so make sure you have at least one of these with you.

IN THIS CHAPTER

» Deciding whether you want texting and calling capabilities

» Picking the best calling, texting, and data option

» Choosing the best data-only option

Chapter **3**
Using Your Cellphone in Japan

Where would we be without smartphones? You may find out the answer to that question when you arrive in Japan and your cellphone doesn't work! If you'd like to have a functioning phone, take a look at some of the different options in this chapter.

Deciding between Data and Voice or Data-Only

There a couple of things you need to take into consideration when deciding how to stay connected while in Japan. The first thing you need to ask yourself is: Do I need voice (phone calls) and messaging (texting), or can I get away with just data (Internet)?

TIP

Many popular apps allow users to make phone calls and send messages through data instead of traditional voice and messaging plans. Facebook Messenger, LINE, Skype, and WhatsApp are just a few. iPhone owners can also use iMessages to send messages and FaceTime to call other iPhone owners using data.

In general, it will likely cost you more to get a plan that will include voice and messaging. If you can get away with just using data, you'll likely save some money. However, sometimes needing to make traditional phone calls just can't be avoided. For example, when I studied abroad in Japan, I needed to call my dorm when I landed to let them know of my expected arrival time.

Choosing the Best Data and Voice Option

If you decide that you need to have calling and texting capabilities, there are two main options for connecting your phone in Japan: Get an international phone plan from your phone provider or pick up a data and voice SIM card in Japan.

International phone plans

The upside of choosing an international phone plan is that your phone will be functional the minute you step off the plane. This is nice because if you need to do a quick Google search on how to navigate the airport, you'll have a phone that can do that. If you go the SIM card route, you have to figure out where to pick it up at the airport or where to buy it at a local store.

TIP

The downside of choosing an international phone plan is that the plans tend to be more expensive — unless you're with Sprint. Sprint offers a $5-per-month add-on that gives you full voice, messaging, and data capabilities while you're in Japan. Just make sure to read the fine print to make sure the data limits will be a good fit for your typical Internet usage. More information about this service can be found at https://shop.sprint.com/global/pdf/shop/japan_roaming_add_on.pdf.

Other phone providers, such as AT&T and Verizon, have a few different options for international travel plans. Both offer a "pay only for the days you use it" option. AT&T calls its plan the International Day Pass; Verizon calls its plan the TravelPass. At the time of writing, both cost $10 per *day* (not per month).

The upside to these is that you get the exact same plan as you have domestically, so if you have unlimited talk, text, and data, that's exactly what you'll have abroad. However, if you plan on visiting Japan for the entire Tokyo 2020 Olympic Games and use your phone every day you're there, you're looking at a bill of about $150.

Other international phone plans range from $60 per month to $130 per month, depending on how many texts you want to send, phone calls you want to place, and surfing of the web you want to do.

Data and voice SIM cards

Unfortunately, most data and voice SIM cards are designed more for long-term visitors to Japan. Many of the data and voice SIM providers have minimum 6- or 12-month contracts and charge hefty fees ($70+) for early cancellation. However, two providers have pay-as-you-go options with no minimum contract: Mobal and Sakura Mobile.

Note that SIM cards come in three different sizes. In the past, you often had to know which size SIM card your phone used before buying one (because you couldn't return it after opening it). Today, most providers just provide you with all three SIM card sizes. Just double-check that this is the case before you buy.

Mobal

Mobal offers only one option for data and voice. However, it also offers an option that is strictly voice and messaging and doesn't include data. Table 3-1 lists both options, but honestly, you'll likely need data to be able to navigate Japan, so I don't recommend choosing the option that is just voice and messaging.

TABLE 3-1 Mobal SIM Card Options

Per Month	Voice and Text	Voice, Text, and Data
Price	¥1,000 ($9.17)*	¥4,500 ($41.28)*
Minutes	Unlimited	Unlimited
Data	N/A	Unlimited**

Incoming calls and texts are always free. Outbound calls to other Mobal SIM card users are free from 1 a.m. to 9 p.m. Outbound calls to other Japanese phones and landlines are an additional ¥29 ($0.26) per minute. Outbound international calls range from ¥65 ($0.59) to ¥200 ($1.83) per minute depending on the country. Outbound domestic texts cost an additional ¥12 ($0.11) per message. Outbound international texts are an additional ¥140 ($1.28) per message.

**Data speeds are reduced significantly after the first 7GB used.*

Also, keep in mind that for Mobal, you have to pay for the SIM card itself separate from the monthly plan. Both SIM card options, as of this writing, cost ¥3,000 ($27.55) for the card.

Sakura Mobile

Sakura Mobile offers four options for data and voice SIM cards (see Table 3-2). Be aware that all these plans have an additional activation fee. The activation fee is typically ¥15,000 ($137.61), but Sakura Mobile often runs discounts where the activation fee is reduced to ¥5,000 ($45.87). Students can get an additional ¥1,000 ($9.17) off the activation fee.

TABLE 3-2 Sakura Mobile SIM Card Options

Per Month	Mini	Standard	Standard+	Big
Price	¥2,980 ($27.35)	¥3,980 ($36.50)	¥4,980 ($45.70)	¥6,680 ($61.30)
Free Minutes*	30 minutes	40 minutes	50 minutes	60 minutes
Data**	3GB	5GB	7GB	20GB

*All plans come with free minutes that can be used for international and domestic calls. Additional minutes cost ¥40 ($0.37) per minute for domestic calls and ¥62 ($0.57) per minute for international calls. Domestic texts cost an additional ¥5 ($0.05) per message. International texts are an additional ¥50 ($0.46) per message.
**Data speeds are reduced significantly if you exceed your monthly data limit.

Choosing the Best Data-Only Option

Data-only will likely be the most affordable option for many people (unless you have Sprint as your phone carrier, in which case see "International phone plans" section, earlier in this chapter). However, there are a couple of different options for getting connected to the Internet while in Japan. Which option is best for you will depend on how frequently you connect to the Internet and how many devices you plan on bringing with you.

Free Wi-Fi

Free Wi-Fi is, as the name suggests, free of charge, and, therefore, the most affordable option for getting connected to the Internet.

There are several places in Japan where you can find free Wi-Fi. Almost all airports and hotels offer free Wi-Fi. Other establishments such as Starbucks and McDonald's offer free Wi-Fi. On occasion, you may even be able to find free Wi-Fi at 7-Eleven convenience stores and at train stations.

TIP

The Japan Wi-Fi app (also called Japan Connected-free WiFi) will display a map of all the hotspot locations where you can get Wi-Fi. The app is available in both the Apple App Store and the Google Play Store.

However, while this option is free, I wouldn't recommend it unless you truly can't afford any of the other options. I relied on my phone heavily when trying to figure out how to get where I wanted to go, especially when trying to navigate the train system (see Chapter 15). Because not all train stations have Wi-Fi, you'll want a phone that can connect to the Internet even when there is no free Wi-Fi available.

Alternatively, you can use this option in conjunction with one of the international phone plans. As mentioned earlier, the most popular international phone plans only charge you for the days you use it, so you can use the international phone plan when absolutely necessary and then just rely on free Wi-Fi locations the rest of the time.

Data-only SIM cards

There are only two main providers for data and voice SIM cards, but there are a lot of providers of data-only SIM cards. Table 3-3 lists a bunch. This list is not exhaustive, but it will at least give you an idea of options and prices. The list is first ordered by duration, and then price. All prices are as of this writing.

TABLE 3-3 Data-Only SIM Card Options

Carrier	Number of Days	Price	Data Limit
SIM Card Geek	5	¥3,480 ($31.92)	Unlimited
eConnect	7	¥1,980 ($18.17)	0.5GB
eConnect	7	¥2,680 ($24.58)	0.7GB
Sakura Mobile	8	¥4,500 ($41.28)	Unlimited

(continued)

TABLE 3-3 *(continued)*

Carrier	Number of Days	Price	Data Limit
TelecomSquare Wi-Ho	8	¥4,980 ($45.69)	Unlimited
B-Mobile	10	¥1,980 ($18.17)	5GB
SIM Card Geek	12	¥4,980 ($45.69)	Unlimited
eConnect	15	¥3,380 ($31.01)	1.5GB
Sakura Mobile	15	¥6,500 ($59.63)	Unlimited
Mobal	16	¥5,990 ($54.95)	Unlimited
B-Mobile	21	¥2,980 ($27.34)	7GB
SIM Card Geek	21	¥6,980 ($64.04)	Unlimited
Wireless Gate	30	¥3,590 ($32.94)	2GB
SIM Card Geek	30	¥4,980 ($45.69)	7GB
Sakura Mobile	30	¥9,000 ($82.57)	Unlimited
TelecomSquare Wi-Ho	31	¥6,980 ($64.04)	Unlimited
Mobal	31	¥7,490 ($68.72)	Unlimited
Wireless Gate	60	¥3,980 ($36.51)	3GB
eConnect	60	¥9,180 ($84.22)	10GB

WARNING

Be aware that most providers have a *fair use policy*, which typically states, "4G LTE speeds are available whenever possible. Please note, however, that data speeds may be restricted during busy times or if large amounts of data are used. If you use more than 3GB of data in a day, your data speeds may be reduced for 24 to 48 hours."

Portable Wi-Fi

Several companies offer portable Wi-Fi. Basically, you're given a compact, portable router that you can carry around with you and use for connecting to the Internet.

This option often works out best for those who are traveling together and have multiple devices that they want to connect to the Internet. For example, if you're a family of four and everybody has a cellphone that he or she wants to be able to use while out and about, portable Wi-Fi will likely be your best option.

It's typically recommended that you reserve a portable Wi-Fi pack at least a couple of days in advance. It will typically be available for pickup at the airport or at your hotel. After you've received the device and password for connecting, all you have to do is switch it on, and it's ready for you to begin using it!

Many different companies offer portable Wi-Fi rentals. Each company advertises different speeds, data allowances, and prices. Table 3-4 lists several portable Wi-Fi options, with all the pertinent details for comparing them, but it isn't an exhaustive list. The list is first ordered by duration, and then by price. All prices are as of this writing.

TABLE 3-4 Portable Wi-Fi Options

Carrier	Price per Day	Number of Days	Data Limit*	Speed (Mbps)
CD Japan–Docomo	¥550 ($5.05)	5	0.2GB	150
CD Japan–Docomo	¥690 ($6.33)	5	0.35GB	150
CD Japan–Cloud Air	¥730 ($6.70)	5	Unlimited	150
Ninja Wifi	¥800 ($7.34)	5	1GB	187.5
CD Japan–Softbank	¥890 ($8.17)	5	Unlimited	187.5
Ninja Wifi	¥900 ($8.26)	5	Unlimited	187.5
Fon Rental WiFi	¥900 ($8.26)	5	Unlimited	612
Fon Rental WiFi	¥1,000 ($9.17)	5	Unlimited	758
Japan Rail Pass	¥1,100 ($10.09)	5	Unlimited	150
Jrailpass	¥1,208 ($11.08)	5	Unlimited	150
CD Japan–Docomo	¥250 ($2.29)	21	0.2GB	150
CD Japan–Docomo	¥320($2.94)	21	0.35GB	150
CD Japan–CloudAir	¥440 ($4.04)	21	Unlimited	187.5
CD Japan–Softbank	¥460 ($4.22)	21	Unlimited	187.5

(continued)

TABLE 3-4 *(continued)*

Carrier	Price per Day	Number of Days	Data Limit*	Speed (Mbps)
Japan Rail Pass	¥524 ($4.81)	21	Unlimited	150
Jrailpass	¥592($5.43)	21	Unlimited	150
Ninja Wifi	¥800 ($7.35)	21	1GB	187.5
Ninja Wifi	¥900 ($8.25)	21	Unlimited	187.5
Fon Rental WiFi	¥900 ($8.25)	21	Unlimited	612
Fon Rental WiFi	¥1,000 ($9.20)	21	Unlimited	758

*Data speeds are reduced significantly if you exceed their fair use policy.

Note that only prices for 5 days and 21 days are listed as points of comparison, but most companies allow you to pick the number of days for which you would like to rent the pocket Wi-Fi.

A downside to portable Wi-Fi packs is that they are yet another device. Unlike using a SIM card, a portable Wi-Fi pack is one more thing you'll have to carry with you on your day-to-day adventures. Plus, it's electronic so you need to make sure it stays charged (although many Wi-Fi pack providers also give you a portable battery with your Wi-Fi pack).

Chapter **4**

What to Bring with You to Japan

nowing what to bring with you to Japan involves more than just grabbing your toothbrush and a few clothes off the hangers. Weather, fashion trends, and cultural norms in Japan will all play a big factor in what you decide to bring with you on your trip.

Knowing What Kind of Weather to Expect

Before you start making your packing list, I first want to go over what the weather is like in Japan, as that will likely affect some of your packing decisions.

In Tokyo, temperatures can get up into the low to mid-90s (°F) in late July and early August. Humidity levels can also get quite higher, so the "feels-like" temperature can get up into the low 100s. Unfortunately, this is the exact same time the Tokyo 2020 Olympics will be held.

If you're from parts of the United States that typically experience high humidity, such as the South and some of the Midwest, Japan's humidity won't be too different from what you're used to at home. However, if you're from the northern or desert areas of the United States, you may find the humidity a bit overwhelming.

Many people take trips to the mountainous areas or more northern parts of Japan where the temperatures and humidity aren't as high, so keep this in mind if you're planning any day trips from Tokyo (see Chapter 17) or other trips around Japan (see Chapter 18). In these areas, average temperatures usually hover closer to the upper 70s and lower 80s. It's still hot, but a bit more bearable.

Packing for Your Trip

For me, packing for a trip is always one of the stressful parts of traveling because I always, without fail, forget at least one important item. I hope this packing list prevents you from doing the same.

Also, keep in mind as you pack that you won't want to pack your suitcases so tight that you can barely close them. There are a lot of different items that make for great souvenirs from Japan. (Don't even ask me how much I spent on souvenirs. I'm too embarrassed to say.) Just know that you'll likely want some extra space in your luggage for anything you pick up along your journey.

Clothes

Loosely fitting clothing will be your best friend. Thankfully, this has also been a fashion trend in Japan of late. Baggy and seemingly oversized clothing is quite popular, which means you'll be able to wear your loose clothing and fit right in!

The other thing to note about fashion in Japan is that Japanese people tend to dress up a bit when stepping out of the house, even if it's just to buy groceries down the street. They're not dressed up as in business-casual "dressed up" (although some people are). However, you definitely won't see people who just rolled out of bed and still are in their pajamas walking around the store either.

Finally, if you have tattoos, you may want to consider clothing that will naturally cover them. Chapter 16 talks more about visiting Japan when you have tattoos, but until you get to that chapter, just know that having clothes that cover any tattoos you may have will likely make your life easier.

Other important items

Sure, clothes are what will take up the most room in your suitcase, but you'll want to bring some other important items with you. In this section, I walk you through a list of these, so you can add relevant items to your packing list.

Documents and money

The items in this section will likely be some of the most important. Most items listed in other sections can be bought in Japan after you arrive, but these items will be essential for your trip.

>> **Passport:** You need this to get into the country. (See Chapter 2 for more information on passports.)

>> **Driver's license (and international driving permit):** Even if you don't plan on doing any driving in Japan, having your driver's license is a good secondary form of identification in addition to your passport. If you do plan on driving, you'll need an international driving permit (more on this in Chapter 15).

>> **Flight, hotel, and Olympic ticket confirmations:** I always prefer to have printed copies of my reservations, especially when in a foreign country. If your phone is dead, having a printed confirmation to show proof of purchase will make your life significantly easier.

>> **Cash:** Cash is king in Japan, so I recommend having at least some Japanese yen on hand when you arrive in Japan. (Check out Chapter 13 for more info on exchanging money before your trip.)

>> **Credit and debit card:** Despite cash being king, some places will accept credit cards. (Again, see Chapter 13 for more info.)

>> **Coin purse:** Japanese currency uses a lot more coins than most Americans are used to. As such, having a small change purse to keep your coins in will definitely be helpful.

>> **Train passes:** Some train passes must be ordered before you arrive in Japan. Just make sure you remember to bring them with you!

>> **SIM card or portable Wi-Fi:** Some companies allow you to reserve SIM cards and portable Wi-Fi so it's ready to go when you land. If you choose to do this, just make sure to bring the confirmation with you. (More on this in Chapter 3.)

Personal items

These are those items from home that you just can't live without. Most of these items you could buy in Japan if you happened to forget them, but I know I would be an unhappy camper if I forgot my favorite shampoo at home.

>> **Travel-size personal care products:** When packing things like shampoo, conditioner, and other personal care products, just keep in mind what you're putting in each bag. TSA has a 3-1-1 rule that states that each passenger can carry on one quart-size, clear bag that can hold 3.4-ounce bottles. Any bottles containing liquids of more than 3.4 ounces will need to go in your checked luggage.

>> **Toothbrush and toothpaste:** Keep in mind that toothpaste is considered a liquid, so it has to go in that clear bag. Plus, don't forget your toothbrush.

>> **Hairbrush or comb:** Does this one need an explanation? If you use a brush or comb on a regular basis, you probably want to bring it with you.

>> **Toiletry bag:** This is particularly useful if you're staying in a hostel or somewhere that has communal showers. Having a small toiletry bag makes it easier for you to carry your stuff to and from the showers.

>> **Sunglasses and sunscreen:** A significant number of the Olympic venues have outdoor seating. As such, you'll likely be in the sun quite a bit during your time in Tokyo. Sunscreen will make sure you don't end up burnt and miserable during your trip. Sunglasses or a hat may also be nice.

>> **Glasses and/or contact solution:** Pretty straightforward. If you wear glasses or contacts, don't forget them at home.

>> **Medications:** You may or may not be able to bring your medications with you. If you're able to bring your medications with you, make sure you actually remember to bring them, as well as any accompanying documentation! See Chapter 2 for more information.

>> **Clothing:** Even if you plan on going to Japan for a couple of weeks, I recommend bringing only a few days' worth of clothing. Bonus points if you can mix and match the clothing. Most hotels have laundry facilities, and when you're ready to leave Japan, you'll be grateful for the extra space you had in your suitcase that wasn't taken up by clothes.

Electronics

Many of these items are essential to ensuring you have a good time in Japan. You'll probably struggle quite a bit without them, and some of them can be quite expensive to buy in Japan if you happen to forget yours at home!

>> **Phone:** I think it's safe to say that you're going to want your cellphone with you in Japan.

>> **Phone charger:** It's not the end of the world if you forget your phone charger, but you probably don't want to spend your first day in Japan walking around an electronics shop looking for a charger because your phone died.

>> **Portable battery:** I highly recommend having at least one of these. You'll likely use your phone quite a bit throughout the day, if only for the GPS and navigating the public transit system. Having a portable battery with you will ensure your phone will be charged when you need it. Depending on the size of your portable battery and how many people are coming with you, you may even want one for each person.

>> **Outlet adapter:** You can find more information about electrical outlets in Japan in Chapter 13. Depending on what type of electronics you bring, you may also want to bring an adapter.

>> **Camera:** Your cellphone camera may be enough, or you may want to bring a "real" camera. Just bring whatever you typically use for taking photos.

In-flight entertainment

The flight to Japan is long. Depending on what time your plane takes off, you may want to sleep on the plane to help you get adjusted to the time difference (see Chapter 13), but that's always easier said than done. Some in-flight essentials can make it a bit easier.

>> **Sleeping items:** Some international flights include pillows and blankets for passengers, but not all, so check your specific flight to see what in-flight amenities are provided. An eye mask and noise-canceling headphones or earplugs will drown out the humming plane engine and help you sleep without all the distractions of happenings on the plane.

>> **Entertainment:** If you can't or don't want to sleep, you'll want something to keep yourself entertained. Some flights offer free movies, but you can only watch so many movies before that gets boring, too. Bringing a deck of cards, a book, podcasts, a journal, and anything else you normally do to entertain yourself can make the flight go by much quicker than just staring at your watch.

Miscellaneous

You know those moments when you're out traveling or just out and about and think to yourself, "Dang! I wish I would've brought that!" That's what you'll be thinking to yourself if you happen to forget any of the following items:

>> **Day bag or purse:** I almost always bring some sort of small bag that I keep on my back when I'm out and about. It's great for keeping things like your camera and souvenirs that you buy along the way.

>> **Hand towel:** You may be surprised to hear (or I guess read in this case) that many restrooms in Japan do *not* have paper towels or dryers. For that reason, many people carry a small hand towel with them for drying their hands.

>> **Travel first-aid kit:** You'll likely do a lot of walking in Japan, especially in Tokyo. It's not uncommon for travelers to report having gotten blisters after doing so much walking their first few days. As such, it's nice to have a small first-aid kit so you aren't trying to figure out how to ask for a Band-Aid in Japanese (which by the way is "Bando-eido").

>> **Card holder:** Most travelers to Japan purchase an IC Card for riding the train (see Chapter 15). It's nice to have a small card holder that can attach to your bag so you don't have to dig out your IC Card every time you want to ride the train or bus.

>> **Guidebooks:** The book you're reading right now? It will be just as useful after you arrive in Japan as when you're preparing for your trip, I promise, so make sure to bring it with you!

The XXXII Olympic Summer Games

Chapter **5**

Venues and Locations

A total of 42 different venues will be used to hold the various events of the Tokyo 2020 Olympics. These venues have been divided into three core areas: the Heritage Zone, the Tokyo Bay Zone, and the Outlying Venues. The locations of these venues will be big factors when you're planning your trip to the Tokyo 2020 Olympics, because they will affect where you decide to stay (see Chapter 10) and how you'll get around the city (see Chapter 15).

TIP

The official Bureau of Tokyo 2020 Olympic and Paralympic Games Preparation recommends using public transportation to get to each of the venues. This means that you'll want to take the train or bus to a nearby station and then either walk or take a shuttle bus to the venue from there.

Chapter 15 contains more information about using the public transit system, but for now just know that you'll need to know what stations are nearby when trying to figure out the best way to get to the venue. In this chapter, I provide a list of nearby stations for each of the venues. You can find more information about getting between the venues and nearby stations on the Tokyo 2020 Olympics website at `https://tokyo2020.org/en/games/venue/olympic`.

Public transit and walkways will be much more crowded than normal during the Olympics, so make sure to allow ample time to get to your destination.

Heritage Zone

The Tokyo 2020 Olympics will actually be the second time Tokyo has hosted the Summer Olympics. The first time Tokyo hosted the Summer Olympics was back in 1964. Many of the venues found within the Heritage Zone are venues that were also used during the 1964 Summer Olympics and are in downtown Tokyo.

Equestrian Park

Address: 2 chōme-1 Kamiyoga, Setagaya City, Tōkyō 158-0098, Japan

Nearest train stations: Chitose–Funabashi Station, Yoga Station

Part of Baji Koen Park, this venue was used to hold the equestrian events during the 1964 Olympics and will again hold the equestrian events including dressage, jumping, and eventing for the 2020 Olympics. Owned by the Japan Racing Authority, the park hosts other equestrian non-Olympics-related training, events, and competitions throughout the year.

Kokugikan Arena

Address: 1-chōme-3-28 Yokoami, Sumida City, Tōkyō-to 130-0015, Japan

Nearest train station: Ryogoku Station

Kokugikan Arena, also known as Ryōgoku Kokugikan or Ryōgoku Sumo Hall, is primarily used for sumo wrestling tournaments. However, it will also be used for other events, such as pro wrestling events and music concerts. During the Tokyo 2020 Olympics, it will be used to hold the various boxing events.

Musashino Forest Sport Plaza

Address: 290-11 Nishimachi, Chofu, Tōkyō-to 182-0032, Japan

Nearest train station: Tobitakyu Station

The Musashino Forest Sport Plaza is a sporting complex with various facilities. The main arena is used for commercial purposes, such as holding sporting events, concerts, and exhibits. It will also be used for the badminton events, as well as the fencing portion of the modern pentathlon. Aside from the main arena, the Musashino Forest Sport Plaza also has a sub-arena that can be used for various indoor sports, indoor swimming, and individual training.

Musashinonomori Park

Address: 3 Chome-5-12 Asahicho, Fuchūichi, Tōkyō-to 183-0003, Japan

Nearest train station: Tama Station

Musashinonomori Park is a public park home to 5,000 trees, a baseball field, and other areas for visitors to hang out and relax. During the Tokyo 2020 Olympics, it will be used as the starting point for the cycling road race.

Nippon Budokan

Address: 2-3 Kitanomarukōen, Chiyoda City, Tōkyō-to 102-8321, Japan

Nearest train station: Kundashita Station

Nippon Budokan, sometimes referred to as just Budokan, was built ahead of the first Tokyo Olympics in 1964 and was originally intended to house martial arts events. Although Nippon Budokan is still used for various judo, kendo, and other martial arts events, it also houses other large-scale events such as concerts. It even housed a Beatles concert back in 1966. The Olympics once again return to Nippon Budokan with the venue being used for the judo and karate events.

Olympic Stadium

Address: 10-1 Kasumigaokamachi, Shinjuku City, Tōkyō-to 160-0013, Japan

Nearest train station: Sendagaya Station

The Olympic Stadium, also referred to as the New National Stadium, replaced the old National Stadium that was used for the 1964 Olympics. The old National Stadium was demolished, and the New National Stadium was built in the same place. For the Tokyo 2020 Olympics, it will be used not only for the track-and-field athletic events, but also for soccer events as well as the opening and closing ceremonies.

Tokyo International Forum

Address: 3-chōme-5-1 Marunouchi, Chiyoda City, Tōkyō-to 100-0005, Japan

Nearest train stations: Yurakucho Station, Tokyo Station

Consisting of a glass atrium plus 4 other buildings, 8 main halls, and a total of 14 stories (3 below ground and 11 above ground), the Tokyo International Forum is Tokyo's first convention and art center. During the Tokyo 2020 Olympics, it will also be home to the weightlifting events.

Tokyo Metropolitan Gymnasium

Address: 1-chōme-17-1 Sendagaya, Shibuya City, Tōkyō-to 151-0051, Japan

Nearest train station: Sendagaya Station

Like many of the other venues being used, the Tokyo Metropolitan Gymnasium is a sporting complex used to hold large-scale sporting events. It also has other facilities typically open to the public, such as a swimming pool and training room, as well as other programs such as yoga, martial arts, and more. In the first Tokyo Olympics in 1964, it was used for gymnastics; it will be used for the table tennis events during the Tokyo 2020 Olympics.

Tokyo Stadium

Address: 376-3 Nishimachi, Chofu, Tōkyō-to 182-0032, Japan

Nearest train station: Tobitakyu Station

Tokyo Stadium, also known as Ajinomoto Stadium, serves as the home field for both the FC Tokyo and Tokyo Verdy soccer teams. In the past, it has also been used for concerts and flea markets.

Most recently, it was used to hold various events for the 2019 Rugby World Cup. For the Tokyo 2020 Olympics, it will be used to host various soccer and rugby events, as well as the swimming, fencing, riding, and laser-run portions of the modern pentathlon.

Yoyogi National Stadium

Address: 2-chōme-1-1 Jinnan, Shibuya City, Tōkyō-to 150-0041, Japan

Nearest train station: Harajuku Station

Also sometimes called the Yoyogi National Gymnasium, the Yoyogi National Stadium was built for the Tokyo Olympics in 1964 and was originally used for the basketball and aquatics events. Since then, it has also been used for the 2006 and 2010 FIVB Women's Volleyball World Championships. The Yoyogi National Stadium returns for the Tokyo 2020 Olympics as a host for the handball events.

Tokyo Bay Zone

As the name implies, many of these venues are located around Tokyo Bay. It's home not only to two popular districts of Tokyo — Ariake and Odaiba — but also to large cities such as Chiba.

Aomi Urban Sports Park

Address: 1 Chome-1 Aomi, Koto City, Tōkyō 135-0064, Japan

Nearest train station: Aomi Station

Aomi Urban Sports Park is one of the few temporary venues for the Tokyo 2020 Olympics. It was traditionally a large parking lot, but it was transformed into a venue capable of hosting the 3x3 basketball and sport climbing events.

Ariake Arena

Address: 2-chōme-2-22 Ariake, Koto City, Tōkyō-to 135-0063, Japan

Nearest train station: Ariake-Tennis-no-mori Station

Ariake Arena is one of the few new venues being built for the Tokyo 2020 Olympics and will host the volleyball events. After the Olympics are over, it will be used as a sporting and cultural center to host various sporting matches, concerts, and other large-scale events.

Ariake Gymnastics Centre

Address: 1-10-1 Ariake, Koto City, Tōkyō-to 135-0063, Japan

Nearest train station: Kokusai-Tenjijō Station, Ariake-Tennis-no-mori Station

The Ariake Gymnastics Centre is unique in that it's a semipermanent venue. It was built to hold the gymnastics events for the Tokyo 2020 Olympics. After the Olympics and Paralympics are over, the venue will be opened as an exhibition hall under the Tokyo Metropolitan Government until 2030.

Ariake Tennis Park

Address: 2-chōme-2-22 Ariake, Koto City, Tōkyō-to 135-0063, Japan

Nearest train station: Kokusai-Tenjijō Station

Originally built in the 1980s, Ariake Tennis Park has been used to host various tennis tournaments and championships. However, it recently underwent renovation to be able to accommodate the tennis events for the Tokyo 2020 Olympics.

Ariake Urban Sports Park

Address: 1 Chome-7 Ariake, Koto City, Tōkyō 135-0063, Japan

Nearest train station: Ariake-Tennis-no-mori Station

Built specifically for the Tokyo 2020 Olympics, the Ariake Urban Sports Park will be used to host the skateboarding events, as well as the BMX racing and BMX freestyle cycling events.

Kasai Canoe Slalom Centre

Address: 6-chōme-1-1 Rinkaichō, Edogawa City, Tōkyō-to 134-0086, Japan

The Kasai Canoe Slalom Centre is the first manmade canoe slalom course in Japan and will be used to hold the canoe slalom events for the Tokyo 2020 Olympics. After the Olympics have completed, the Centre will become available for other canoe competitions.

Makuhari Messe Hall

Address: 2-1, Nakase, Mihama-ku, Chiba City, Chiba-ken 261-0023, Japan

Nearest train station: Kaihimmakuhari Station

Makuhari Messe Hall is a large convention center that consists of three main zones: the International Exhibition Hall, the International Conference Hall, and the Makuhari Event Hall. Rooms 1 through 8 in the International Conference Hall are also referred to as Hall A and will be used to host the tae kwon do and wrestling events during the Olympics. Rooms 9 through 11 of the International Conference Hall are referred to as Hall B and will hold the Olympic fencing events.

Odaiba Marine Park

Address: 1-chōme-4-1 Daiba, Minato City, Tōkyō-to 135-0091, Japan

Nearest train station: Daiba Station

Odaiba Marine Park gives visitors access to the Tokyo waterfront. Swimming is not allowed, but other sports such as windsurfing can be practiced here. It's also home to a replica of the Statue of Liberty, and it provides views of the famous Rainbow Bridge. During the Tokyo 2020 Olympics, it will be used as a temporary venue for the marathon swimming and triathlon events.

Oi Hockey Stadium

Address: 4-chōme-1-19 Yashio, Shinagawa City, Tōkyō-to 140-0003, Japan

Nearest train station: Oi Keibajo Mae Station

Oi Hockey Stadium, built in the Oi Pier Ocean Park, is one of the new venues being built for the Tokyo 2020 Olympics and will be used to host the hockey events. It's also one of the most sustainable Olympic venues in history due to the fact that 60 percent of the turf is made from sugar cane, meaning that it will need two-thirds less water than previous Olympic turfs. After the Olympics, the stadium will be used for other future sporting events.

Sea Forest Cross-Country Course

Address: 3-chome, Aomi, Koto-ku, Tōkyō-to 135-0064, Japan

Nearest train stations: Tokyo Teleport Station, Shin-kiba Station

The Sea Forest Cross-Country Course is another one of the temporary venues that will be used to host the cross-country equestrian events during the Tokyo 2020 Olympics. After the conclusion of the Games, the area will be opened up as a park for public use.

Sea Forest Waterway

Address: 3-chome, Aomi, Koto-ku, Tōkyō-to 135-0064, Japan

Nearest train stations: Tokyo Teleport Station, Shin-kiba Station

Just next to the Sea Forest Park is the Sea Forest Waterway, which will be used for the canoe sprint events, as well as the rowing events during the Tokyo 2020 Olympics events. Afterward, it will continue to be used for other rowing and canoeing competitions.

Shiokaze Park

Address: 1 Higashiyashio, Shinagawa City, Tōkyō 135-0092, Japan

Nearest train stations: Daiba Station, Fune-no-kagakukan Station

Shiokaze Park is the largest park in the Tokyo waterfront area and a popular place for friends and families to hang out. Visitors can have a picnic and enjoy the great views of Tokyo Bay. During the Olympics, it will also be used as a temporary venue for the beach volleyball events.

Tatsumi Water Polo Centre

Address: 2-chōme-8-10 Tatsumi, Koto City, Tōkyō-to 135-0053, Japan

The Tokyo Tatsumi International Swimming Center, being referred to as the Tatsumi Water Polo Centre, will be used for — you guessed it — the water polo events for the Tokyo 2020 Olympics. Outside the Olympics, it has also been used to host various swimming competitions.

Tokyo Aquatics Centre

Address: 2 Chome-2 Tatsumi, Koto City, Tōkyō 135-0053, Japan

Nearest train stations: Tatsumi Station, Shiomi Station

The Tokyo Aquatics Centre, also referred to as the Olympics Aquatic Centre, is one of the new venues being built for the Olympics. During the Tokyo 2020 Olympics, it will be used for the swimming, artistic swimming, and diving events. After the Olympics, it will be used for other aquatic competitions.

Yumenoshima Park Archery Field

Address: 2 Chome-1 Yumenoshima, Koto City, Tōkyō 136-0081, Japan

Nearest train station: Shin-kiba Station

Also called Dream Island Archery Field, this archery field was constructed inside Yumenoshima Park in order to be able to host the Tokyo 2020 Olympics archery events. After the Olympics, it will be used to host archery tournaments and workshops, as well as other recreational activities.

Outlying Venues

Aptly named, venues that are not located in either the Heritage Zone or Tokyo Bay Zone are referred to as the Outlying Venues. Many of the outlying venues are existing sporting stadiums used for sports such as baseball and soccer. Other outlying venues were chosen because certain sports, such as surfing, have specific requirements or needs that couldn't satisfied by a venue within either the Heritage Zone or the Tokyo Bay Zone.

Some of these venues are located in areas such as Saitama and Yokohama, which are just outside of Tokyo. From downtown Tokyo, it typically takes anywhere from 30 minutes to an hour to get there during nonpeak travel times. Other venues are as far as Miyagi and Sapporo. Even on the bullet train, it can take as long as two and a half hours to get to Miyagi from Tokyo and up to nine hours to get to Sapporo. As such, I highly recommend looking at the locations of these venues before finalizing your accommodations in Japan (see Chapter 10) and determining how you'll get around (see Chapter 15).

Asaka Shooting Range

Address: 9 Chome-4 Oizumigakuencho, Nerima City, Tōkyō 178-0061, Japan

Nearest train station: Wakoshi Station

Asaka Shooting Range is one of the few venues used in the first Tokyo Olympics in 1964 that is not located within the Heritage Zone. Instead, it's located in Asaka City, just outside of Tokyo. As in the 1964 Olympics, the Asaka Shooting Range will be used for all shooting-related events. Outside of the Olympics, it's used by the Japan Rifle Shooting Association, as well as by members of the Physical Training School from the Japan Ground Self-Defence Force (JGSDF) Asaka army post.

Enoshima Yacht Harbour

Address: 1-chōme-12-2 Enoshima, Fujisawa, Kanagawa 251-0036, Japan

Nearest train station: Katase-Enoshima Station

Enoshima Yacht Harbour is another one of the legacy venues from the 1964 Olympics and is also Japan's first harbor capable of hosting watersports competitions. During the Tokyo 2020 Olympics, it will be used to host the sailing events.

Fuji International Speedway

Address: 694 Nakahinata, Oyama, Suntō-gun, Shizuoka 410-1307, Japan

Nearest train stations: Suruga-Oyama Station, Gotemba Station

Just outside Mt. Fuji, the Fuji International Speedway, sometimes shortened to just Fuji Speedway, will be used for the cycling individual, as well as the finish line for the cycling road race, during the Tokyo 2020 Olympics.

Fukushima Azuma Baseball Stadium

Address: Kamikotoba-1 Sabara, Fukushima, 960-2158, Japan

Nearest train station: JR Fukushima Station

Fukushima Azuma Baseball Stadium will be one of the venues used to host the baseball and softball events during the Tokyo 2020 Olympics. It will host the first baseball event, as well as six of the softball events.

Ibaraki Kashima Stadium

Address: 26-2 Atoyama, Jinkōji, Kashima, Ibaraki 314-0007, Japan

Nearest train station: Kashima-Soccer Stadium Station

Ibaraki Kashima Stadium is one of the seven venues being used for soccer events during the Tokyo 2020 Olympics. It's a dedicated soccer stadium that serves as the home field for the Kashima Antlers professional soccer team. It also hosted a handful of the 2002 FIFA World Cup matches.

International Stadium Yokohama

Address: 3300 Kozukuechō, Kohoku Ward, Yokohama, Kanagawa 222-0036, Japan

Nearest train station: Shin-Yokohama Station

Also known as Nissan Stadium, the International Stadium Yokohama is another one of the venues being used for soccer events during the Tokyo 2020 Olympics. It's also the largest stadium in Japan, with a seating capacity of 70,000+. Over the years, it has been used to host FIFA World Cup and Rugby World Cup matches, as well as other large-scale events.

Izu MTB Course

Address: 1826 Ono, Izu, Shizuoka 410-2402, Japan

Nearest train station: Shuzenji Station

Despite being about 75 miles from downtown Tokyo, Izu is home to Japan's Cycle Sport Center, which offers various areas and routes for cyclists of all experience levels. Just adjacent is the off-road course that will be used to host the mountain bike cycling events for the Tokyo 2020 Olympics.

Izu Velodrome

Address: 1826 Ono, Izu, Shizuoka 410-2402, Japan

Nearest train station: Shuzenji Station

Also located at Japan's Cycle Sport Center is the Izu Velodrome, which will be used to host the track cycling events during the Tokyo 2020 Olympics. It contains an indoor 250-meter wooden cycling track and has been used to host various cycling competitions, including the Asian Cycling Championships and the Japan Track Cup.

Kasumigaseki Country Club

Address: 3398 Kasahata, Kawagoe City, Saitama 350-1175, Japan

Nearest train station: Kasahata Station

Founded in 1929, the Kasumigaseki Country Club has hosted several golf competitions over the years, including the Canada Cup (World Cup of Golf), Japan Open Golf Championship, and Asia-Pacific Amateur Championship. The Country Club contains two courses: the West Course and the East Course. For the Tokyo 2020 Olympics, the East Course will be used to host the golfing events.

It's also worth noting that until 2017, the rules of the Kasumigaseki Country Club prohibited women from playing on Sundays. However, after many critics argued that the club's policy contradicted the Olympic charter (guaranteeing that individuals have a right to practice a sport without discrimination), the International Olympic Committee (IOC) threatened to remove the club's status as a venue for the Tokyo 2020 Olympics. In March 2017, the Kasumigaseki

Country Club board overturned the restrictions on female membership and granted women full membership rights.

Miyagi Stadium

Address: Tate-40-1 Sugaya, Rifu, Miyagi-gun, Miyagi 981-0122, Japan

Nearest train stations: Shin-Rifu Station, Rifu Station

Also called Hitomebore Stadium Miyagi, Miyagi Stadium is another venue to be used for hosting the soccer events during the Tokyo 2020 Olympics. It has also hosted both men's and women's FIFA World Cup matches and is most known for its crescent moon roof, inspired by the famous Date Masamune, a feudal lord of historic Japan.

Saitama Stadium

Address: 2-chome-1 Misono, Midori Ward, Saitama, 336-0967, Japan

Nearest train station: Urawa-Misono Station

Saitama Stadium is the second largest stadium in Japan and the largest dedicated soccer stadium in Japan. It was originally built to host events for the 2002 FIFA World Cup and now serves as the home field for the Urawa Red Diamonds soccer team. During the Tokyo 2020 Olympics, it will be used to host some of the soccer events.

Saitama Super Arena

Address: 8 Shintoshin, Chuo Ward, Saitama, 330-9111, Japan

Nearest train station: Saitama-Shintoshin Station

Saitama Super Arena is one of Japan's largest multipurpose venues. Its moving block architecture system allows it to transform into an arena, stadium, and exhibit hall, seating anywhere from 6,000 to 37,000 guests. During the Tokyo 2020 Olympics, the venue will be used to host the basketball events.

Sapporo Dome

Address: 1 Hitsujigaoka, Toyohira Ward, Sapporo, Hokkaido 062-0045, Japan

Nearest train station: Fukuzumi Station

By far the farthest venue from downtown Tokyo, Sapporo Dome is located on Hokkaido, Japan's northernmost island. It can be transformed to host both baseball games and soccer and rugby matches. It has been used as a venue for the 2002 FIFA World Cup and is also home to both the Hokkaido Nippon-Ham Fighters baseball team and the Hokkaido Consadole Sapporo soccer team. During the Tokyo 2020 Olympics, it will be one of the many venues being used for the soccer matches.

Sapporo Odori Park

Address: 7-chome Odorinishi, Chuo Ward, Sapporo, Hokkaido 060-0042, Japan

Nearest train stations: Odori Station, Sapporo Station

The race walk was originally scheduled to be held at the Imperial Palace Garden, and the marathon was scheduled to be held at the Olympic Stadium. However, due to concerns around the heat and humidity in Tokyo and the athletes' safety, the International Olympic Committee (IOC) decided to move the events to Sapporo Odori Park, approximately nine hours north of Tokyo by bullet train. When not hosting Olympic events, Sapporo Odori hosts some of the other popular seasonal events unique to Sapporo, such as the Snow Festival, Lilac Festival, and YOSAKOI Soran Festival.

Tsurigasaki Surfing Beach

Address: 6961-1 Torami, Ichinomiya, Chōsei-gun, Chiba 299-4303, Japan

Nearest train station: Kazusa-Ichinomiya Station

Tsurigasaki Surfing Beach is a popular surfing area located in Chiba, about 40 miles from Tokyo. It's known for its world-class waves — it attracts about 600,000 surfers every year. It's no surprise then that this popular surfing beach was chosen to be the venue for the surfing events debuting for the first time at the Tokyo 2020 Olympics.

Yokohama Baseball Stadium

Address: Yokohamakoen, Naka Ward, Yokohama, Kanagawa 231-0022, Japan

Nearest train station: Kannai Station

Built in 1978, Yokohama was the first multipurpose stadium in Japan. It is primarily used for baseball games and is home to the Yokohama DeNa Baystars baseball team. It will also be used to host baseball and softball events during the Tokyo 2020 Olympics.

Chapter **6**

Understanding the Games

You may already be relatively familiar with some of the Olympic sports, like baseball and basketball (although no judgment here if you're not). However, you may not know too much about other sports, including those making their debut at the 2020 Olympics. If you need a crash course on one of the sports, read on!

Opening and Closing Ceremonies

Okay, these aren't actually sports, but they're ticketed events that tend to get thrown in with the list of sports, so I'm covering them here.

As I'm sure you can guess by the name, an opening ceremony is held at the beginning of the Olympics, and a closing ceremony is held after all the Olympic events are over. These ceremonies are often a big show, celebrating the host country's culture, history, and achievements, as well promoting the removal of barriers based on nationality and ethnic backgrounds.

During the opening ceremony, delegates from each country parade around the stadium track, with one person bearing the country's flag (which is considered a great honor). Other important rituals held during the opening ceremony include the declaration of the official opening of the Games, the raising of the Olympic flag, and recitation of the Olympic oath. Then comes the most anticipated part of the opening ceremony: the lighting of the Olympic flame by the torch bearer.

During the closing ceremonies, a bouquet of flowers is handed to a representative of the volunteers, thanking all the volunteers for their hard work. Also, the official Olympic flag is lowered and passed to the mayor of the city that will next host the Olympic Games. Athletes, wearing the medals they won during their respective competitions, then come together in celebration, creating a party-like atmosphere.

Aquatics

You may be surprised to learn that many of the different aquatic events, such as artistic swimming and diving, aren't actually sports but *disciplines,* or branches of the sport known as *aquatics.* The sport of aquatics contains a total of five disciplines: artistic swimming, diving, marathon swimming, swimming, and water polo.

Artistic swimming

There are two parts to artistic swimming:

>> **The technical routine:** The technical routine can last a maximum of 2 minutes and 50 seconds and must contain at least five designated movements.

>> **The free routine:** The free routine doesn't have any required movements and typically last 3 to 4 minutes.

For this sport, athletes can compete in duets or teams. Performances are scored based on synchronization, difficulty, technique, and choreography.

Diving

Diving has two different competitions:

>> **Springboard:** For the springboard, athletes jump from a diving board that bounces, "springing" athletes into the air.

>> **Platform:** The platform dive is done from a fixed platform that doesn't move.

For both the springboard and platform competitions, there are individual events (where there is only one diver) and synchronized events (where two divers dive at the same time, in unison). Dives are scored based on the execution of the diver's movements, as well as the lack of splash when entering the water. For the synchronized events, how well the divers manage to stay synchronized is also a factor in the scoring.

Marathon swimming

Marathon swimming is a 10-kilometer (6.2-mile) race to the finish. It typically takes around two hours to complete. It's usually held in open water (such as seas and lakes) as opposed to indoor aquatic arenas, so athletes have to overcome changing swimming conditions such as waves and currents.

Swimming

In traditional swimming events, athletes race to the finish line, aiming to be the person with the fastest completion time. There are different events based on the stroke used for the race and length of the race. The different strokes are backstroke, breaststroke, butterfly, and freestyle. Lengths of the races can range anywhere from 50 meters to 1,500 meters. There are also the medley events, where athletes use all four strokes over the course of the race. Finally, there are relay events where athletes work as a team, switching between swimmers for different legs of the race.

Water polo

Water polo is played in teams of seven, with the objective being to get the ball into the opponent's goal. The game is played in a large pool, meaning that players have to stay afloat for the duration of the game (although substitutions are allowed). Like many other sports, the game is divided into four quarters, each lasting eight minutes. Teams are only allowed to have possession of the ball for 30 seconds, meaning that they must try to score a goal within 30 seconds of gaining possession of the ball; otherwise, possession goes to the other team. To make it harder, players other than the goalie are only allowed to touch the ball with one hand.

Archery

In archery, athletes use bows and arrows in an attempt to hit the center of a target 70 meters (230 feet) away and score the most points. The number of points scored is based on how close athletes come to hitting the center of the target. The targets have a total diameter of 122 centimeters (4 feet), but the center circle that awards the full ten points is only about 12.2 centimeters (4¾ inches) in width, which is approximately the size of a CD.

Athletics

Like aquatics, athletics is sort of an umbrella sport. It contains five different athletic disciplines: marathon, race walk, track and field, the decathlon, and the heptathlon.

Marathon

The marathon discipline is a long-distance race that is held on average roads. It's 42.195 kilometers (26.2 miles) long and typically takes a little over two hours for the best athletes to complete.

Race walk

What differentiates race walking from traditional running events is the rule that at least one foot must be in contact with the ground at all times. From the time the foot comes in contact with the ground to the time the leg is in its upright position, the knee cannot be bent. Basically, as you step forward, you cannot bend your knee until you're ready to take another step again. The women's race walk event is 20 kilometers (12.43 miles) long, and the men's race is 50 kilometers (31.07 miles).

Track and field

The athletic discipline of track and field consists of a variety of different events. Some of the track events are standard races for short, middle, or long distances around a track. Other track events involve jumping over obstacles or trading off between team members. Field events, which are held inside or outside the track, include high jump, pole vaulting, long jump, shot put, and more.

Decathlon

The decathlon is an event specifically for men where athletes compete in ten different sports:

» 100-meter run

» Long jump

» Shot put

» High jump

» 400-meter run

» 110-meter hurdles

» Discus throw

» Pole vault

» Javelin throw

» 1,500-meter run

Each sport has its own scoring table, and competitors earn points based on their performance in each of the sports. The athlete to accumulate the most points at the end of all the competitions is the winner.

Heptathlon

The heptathlon is an event specifically for women where athletes compete in seven different sports:

» 100-meter hurdles

» High jump

» Shot put

» 200-meter run

» Long jump

>> Javelin throw

>> 800-meter run

Each sport has its own scoring table, and competitors earn points based on their performance in each of the sports. The athlete to accumulate the most points at the end of all the competitions is the winner.

Badminton

In badminton, athletes use lightweight rackets to hit the shuttlecock, a round cork with cone-shaped feathers, into the opponent's side of the court. A match consists of three games and is won by winning at least two of the three games. A game is won by being the first to reach 21 points.

Baseball/softball

A baseball field consists of the infield and outfield. The infield has four bases: first, second, third, and home. For the team that is up to bat, athletes start at home base and attempt to get around all the bases and return to home. Athletes get a chance to make their way to the next base when they or one of their teammates uses a baseball bat to hit the ball that is *pitched* (thrown) to them. The opposing team is in the field and attempts to retrieve the ball that was hit and get it to the base the player is running to before the player can arrive at the base. If the ball arrives at the base before the runner or the runner is tagged by one of the opposing players who has possession of the ball, that runner is out. A point is scored if a player manages to make it back to home base without getting out.

Teams take turns being up to bat and being in the field, switching after the team that is up to bat has received three outs. One complete rotation is referred to as an *inning*. The game is won by having the most points at the end of nine innings.

Softball, one of the new sports in the Tokyo 2020 Olympics (it had been in previous Olympics, but was absent for the last few Olympic Games), is incredibly similar to baseball in terms of gameplay and rules. The biggest difference is that softball fields are often smaller, and in softball the ball is pitched to the batter underhanded instead of overhanded.

Basketball

You're probably familiar with basketball, but did you know that the Summer Olympics actually has two different types of basketball events? The sport of basketball actually contains two disciplines: traditional basketball and 3x3 basketball.

Traditional basketball

Traditional basketball is played with teams of five players. The object is to get the ball into the net or basket. Games are divided into four quarters, each lasting ten minutes.

Points are awarded depending on what kind of *shot* (throw at the basket) players make. Shots made from behind the three-point line on the court are awarded — you guessed it — three points. Shots made from in front of this line during normal gameplay are awarded two points. Shots made from the free-throw line, which usually happens after a penalty has occurred, are worth one point. The challenge in basketball is that players who have possession of the ball must *dribble* the ball (bounce it on the court repeatedly) in order to be able to move around the court.

3x3 basketball

Unlike traditional basketball, 3x3 basketball is played with teams of three players instead of teams of five. A game ends after ten minutes or after a team has scored 21 points. Scoring in 3x3 basketball is also slightly different from traditional basketball. Instead of having a three-point line, there is a two-point line. Shots made from behind this line are worth two points, and shots made from in front of it are worth one point.

Boxing

The objective of boxing is relatively straightforward: Land more successful blows to your opponent's head and torso than your opponent lands on you. A boxing match consists of three rounds, each being three minutes long. Judges award points to the boxers when they see successful hits. Matches can end in a couple of different scenarios:

>> The referee ends the match due to a significant difference in points.

>> A doctor indicates that the match should be stopped.

>> A player is disqualified after receiving three penalties.

>> A player is unable to resume fighting within ten seconds of being hit.

Canoe

Two different disciplines fall under the umbrella sport of canoeing: slalom and sprint. Both are races, but they're differentiated by the setup of the race.

Slalom

In slalom events, the white-water rapids course has different gates that the athlete must pass through as he makes his way through the course. The idea is to complete the course as quickly as possible, but touching one of the gates adds a 2-second time penalty, and missing a gate altogether adds a 50-second time penalty.

Sprint

The sprint discipline of canoe is a standard race of who can finish first. In this discipline, all athletes are competing at the same time on a straight, flat-water course to be the first one to cross the finish line.

Cycling

The Summer Olympics encompasses many different types of cycling — five to be exact. It contains two bicycle moto cross (BMX) disciplines: freestyle and racing. Outside of BMX, the other disciplines are mountain bike, road, and track.

BMX freestyle

This event is brand new and will be making its debut in the Tokyo 2020 Olympics. In this event, athletes create a routine, or *run,* that lasts for 60 seconds and showcases their skill and creativity. Similar to other freestyle-type events, athletes are judged based on difficulty, creativity, execution, and overall composition.

BMX racing

In the BMX racing event, the course contains a series of jumps and banked corners, as well as some straight and flat areas. Athletes begin the race from an 8-meter-high (26.25-foot) ramp and try to be the first one to cross the finish line.

Mountain bike

The mountain bike events are standard race-to-the-finish types of competitions. However, what sets them apart is the fact that the course is made of rough terrain, full of various ascents, descents, and other naturally occurring elements that make the course tough to navigate.

Road

The road race is a long-distance cycling race completed on a standard street. The men's race spans a distance of 234 kilometers (145.4 miles) for the Tokyo Summer Olympics and takes approximately six hours to complete, while the women's race is 137 kilometers (85.13 miles) long and takes approximately four hours to complete.

There is also an individual time-trial event, where riders race against the clock (as opposed to each other). The men's individual time trial is roughly 50 kilometers (31 miles) and the women's is roughly 30 kilometers (18.6 miles).

Track

The track discipline involves races held on a typical racetrack and has several different events:

>> **Sprint:** This event is a standard race to the finish.

>> **Madison:** This event is a type of relay race.

>> **Keirin:** In this event, a motorcycle is on the track and sets pace for the riders for half the race before leaving, allowing riders to sprint for the finish.

>> **Team pursuit:** In this event, two teams start on opposite sides of the tracks and whoever finishes first or manages to catch the other team is the winner.

>> **Omnium:** This event consists of a combination of four separate events:

- **Scratch race:** The scratch race is similar to the sprint event and is a race to the finish.

- **Tempo race:** In the tempo race, points are awarded to the athlete in first place at the end of each lap.

- **Elimination race:** For the elimination race, the rider in last place at the end of every two laps gets eliminated.

- **Points race:** In the points race, athletes are awarded points throughout a 20-kilometer (12.43-mile) to 25-kilometer (15.53-mile) race.

Equestrian

The equestrian sport is one of the only sports in the Olympics where men and women go head-to-head instead of having separate competitions. It's also the only Olympic sport that involves animals. It contains three different disciplines: dressage, eventing, and jumping.

Dressage

Dressage is considered to be the foundation for all other equestrian disciplines. In dressage, the rider must demonstrate her ability to have the horse do a series of required movements, whether it be galloping, changing direction, moving side to side, or other commands. Each movement is given a score out of 10 points, and at the end, all the points are added together to calculate a percentage. The rider with the highest percentage wins.

Jumping

In the jumping competitions, the rider directs his horse through an obstacle course and has the horse jump over several obstacles (such as triple bars, stone walls, and pools of water). If the horse fails to clear an obstacle or misses it completely, the rider is given a penalty. The rider with the fewest penalties and fastest course completion time is the winner.

Eventing

Eventing is a combination of both dressage and jumping, as well as a third event called cross-country. The jumping event tests the technical jumping skills, but the cross-country event tests the rider and horse's endurance and stamina. The cross-country course can be up to 6.44 kilometers (4 miles) long and have up to 40 different obstacles to jump. The rider with the least total points deducted wins.

Fencing

Like many combat-based sports, the goal of fencing is to strike your opponent without letting her strike you. The key difference in fencing from other combat sports is that a sword is used to strike opponents instead of hands and feet.

Fencing has three main different competitions: foil, épée, and sabre. They vary by the weapon used, valid target area, and priority.

Golf

The objective of golf is to use golf clubs to get a golf ball into the designated hole in the least number of hits, or *strokes,* as possible. One golf round is made up of 18 different courses with one hole each. Four rounds are played over four days for a total of 72 holes. At the end of the 72 holes, the winner is the athlete with the least number of strokes.

Gymnastics

Gymnastics has a total of three disciplines: artistic, rhythmic, and trampoline. All these disciplines demonstrate the athlete's strength, balance, finesse, flexibility, and athleticism in their own ways.

Artistic

In artistic gymnastics, different events involve athletes performing short routines with different equipment, such as rings, the pommel horse, the balance beam, or other items. There is also a floor routine competition, which is done on an open floor instead of with a specific piece of equipment. Scores are awarded based on the complexity and flow of the routine, as well as execution of the individual techniques.

Rhythmic

Similar to artistic gymnastics, in rhythmic gymnastics, female athletes perform various routines. However, in rhythmic gymnastics, athletes perform to music and can use additional props such as hoops, balls, clubs, and ribbons. In individual routines, performances must be 75 to 90 seconds long, and team performances must be 135 to 150 seconds long.

Trampoline

Trampoline gymnastics is another routine-based event, but in this sport, athletes use trampolines to give them enough height to be able to perform several twists, bounces, and somersaults in the air. Scores are awarded based on the difficulty and execution of techniques, as well as total air time.

Handball

Handball is played in teams of seven (one goalie and six outfielders), with the objective being to get the ball into the opponent's goal. Games are divided into two halves, each lasting for 30 minutes. When a player gets possession of the ball, he can hang on to the ball for a maximum of 3 seconds. While a player has possession of the ball, he can dribble the ball and take up to three steps when not dribbling.

Hockey

For many people, when somebody says "hockey," the first thing that comes to mind is ice hockey. However, ice hockey is part of the Winter Olympics. For the Summer Olympics, the sport of hockey refers to field hockey.

The general objective of field hockey and ice hockey are the same: to use a curved stick to strike an object into the opponent's goal. However, there are many differences between field hockey and ice hockey. The first and likely most obvious is that field hockey is played on a traditional sports field, whereas ice hockey is played on ice. Another notable difference is that field hockey uses a ball instead of a puck. Also, in field hockey, teams consist of 11 players (instead of 6) and games are divided into four quarters, each lasting 15 minutes.

Judo

Judo is one of the martial arts that will be held during the Summer Olympics. However, unlike other martial arts whose objective is to land as many hits on the opponent as possible, the object of judo is to subdue an opponent on the ground and force him to submit. Various levels of points are awarded for technique, lengths of pins, and other demonstrated skills.

Karate

Karate, one of the new sports for the Tokyo 2020 Olympics, has two different types of competitions:

>> **Kata (forms):** In the kata competitions, athletes perform a sequence of movements and are scored based on rhythm, speed, power, and balance.

>> **Kumite (sparring):** In kumite competitions, which are divided out by weight class, athletes try to kick, punch, and strike their opponents in order to score points. The athlete with the most points at the end of the three-minute match wins.

Modern Pentathlon

The modern pentathlon is considered to be a test of all-around prowess and consists of five different events that all athletes must compete in:

>> **Fencing ranking:** In the fencing ranking round, athletes compete in round-robin matches, trying to accumulate points.

>> **Fencing bonus:** The fencing bonus round is based off the results of the fencing ranking round and allows victorious athletes to add one point to their scores from the ranking round.

>> **Swimming:** In the swimming round, competitors are awarded points based on their finishing times of a 200-meter race.

>> **Riding:** For the riding event, athletes must complete an equestrian jumping course with a horse that the riders have never ridden before and receive points based on their finishing times.

>> **Laser run:** The laser run involves completing different circuits consisting of shooting laser pistols at several targets and running for a specific distance.

Rowing

Part of what makes rowing so fascinating is that it's one of the only sports where athletes are facing backward when they cross the finish line. As in canoeing, athletes use oars to propel a boat forward. However, in rowing, athletes sit in the boats facing backward and have seats that move forward and backward as they use the oars.

There are two main types of rowing competitions:

>> **Scull:** In scull events, athletes hold one oar in each hand. These events are further divided out into single sculls, double sculls, and quadruple sculls (referring to the number of people in the boat). There are also lightweight events, which have specific rules around the weights of the athletes.

>> **Sweep:** In sweep events, athletes use both hands to hold a single oar. These events are divided out into pairs, fours, and eights (again referring to the number of people in the boat).

Rugby

The object of rugby is simple: Score points by getting the rugby ball to the opponent's goal line. However, depending on the scoring method used, different points are awarded:

>> **Try (5 points):** The player grounds the ball on or after the opponent's try line but before the dead-ball line.

>> **Conversion (2 points):** After a "try" is scored, the team gets an opportunity to score additional points by kicking at the goal.

>> **Drop goal (3 points):** The player kicks the ball after it bounces over the goal posts.

>> **Penalty goal (3 points):** Players who have been awarded a penalty are given the opportunity to kick at the goal.

Another rule to note also happens to be one of the unique aspects of rugby: Players can only pass the ball backward. They can't pass the ball to players who are already farther down the field.

Sailing

Sailing has a total of six different types of competitions. The different types of events refer to the different types of boats used in the event:

>> **Laser and Laser Radial:** A one-person dinghy (Laser is for the men's events and Laser Radial is for the women's).

>> **Finn:** A one-person heavyweight dinghy.

>> **470:** A two-person dinghy.

>> **49er and 49erFX:** A two-person high-performance skiff (49er is for the men's events and 49erFX is for the women's).

>> **RS:X:** A sail board.

>> **Nacra 17:** A multihull catamaran.

Each event consists of multiple races, with competitors scoring points at the end of each race. Unlike other sports, the objective of sailing is to have the *least* amount of points (instead of the most amount of points). For standard races, the winner of the race is given one point. The second-place finisher is given two points, and so on. The final race, or medal race, has double points. The competitor with the least amount of points at the end of all the races is the winner.

Shooting

The sport of shooting is divided into two different disciplines, with each focusing on different shooting styles and weapons.

Rifle and pistol

In the rifle and pistol discipline, a total of four different guns are used: rifle, air rifle, rapid-fire pistol, and air pistol. The goal is to hit as close to the center of the target as possible. The events are divided out not only by the gun the competitors are using, but also by the distance from which they're shooting. There are also three different shooting positions:

>> **Kneeling:** Athletes rest the gun on one knee while keeping the other knee on the ground.

>> **Prone:** Athletes lie on the ground and prop themselves up on their elbows to shoot.

>> **Standing:** Athletes stand in an upright position for shooting.

Shotgun

In the shotgun discipline, athletes use — you guessed it — shotguns for shooting. Unlike the rifle and pistol discipline, the goal in shotgun events is to hit a flying plate, called a *clay*. There are two main types of shotgun events:

>> **Trap:** In trap events, the clay is thrown from a single trap from a long distance away.

>> **Skeet:** In skeet events, the clay is thrown from traps on both the right and left.

Skateboarding

When you think of a skatepark, what comes to mind? Do you picture a park that has a big hole in the ground with lots of twists and curves? Or do you picture a wide-open street-like area full of steps, guardrails, benches, and other items? Congratulations! You just discovered the difference between the two disciplines of skateboarding, one of the new Olympic sports.

Park

The park discipline of skateboarding is held in a hollowed-out area in the ground. From the center, the sides begin to rise quickly, with the top part being almost (if not exactly) a 90-degree angle, meaning it's straight up and down. The curves, as well as sharp inclines, allow skaters to attain relatively quick speeds, as well as achieve significant height above the top rim as they make their way around the course. Points are awarded to the skater based on height, speed, difficulty, stability, and timing, as well as overall composition of the tricks performed.

Street

As mentioned earlier, the street discipline takes part of a course designed to contain the various items that you may come across on your average street that skateboarders can use to do tricks on. Like park skateboarding, scores for the street competition are awarded based on the difficulty, height, speed, and originality of the tricks, as well as flow of the performance.

Soccer

Soccer is played in teams of 11. One game consists of two halves, each 45 minutes long. Like many sports, the objective of the game is to get the ball into the opponent's goal, and the game is won by scoring more points than your opponent. However, in soccer, the only players on the field who can touch the ball with their hands are the goalies. All the players on the field can only use their head, chest, knees, and feet to touch the ball and get it across the field to the opponent's goal.

Sport Climbing

Sport climbing is another one of the new sports making its debut at the Tokyo Olympics. Unless you're an avid sport-climbing fan, chances are this sport will be as new to you as it will be to the Olympics.

Similar to the triathlon, sport climbing combines three different events into one:

>> **Speed climbing:** In this event, two competitors race to the top of a 15-meter-high (49-foot) wall.

>> **Bouldering:** In this event, competitors attempt to complete as many fixed routes as possible on a 4-meter-high (13-foot) wall within four minutes without the use of safety ropes and cords, just climbing shoes and chalk for the hands.

>> **Lead climbing:** In this event, lead climbers try to climb as high as possible in six minutes. In lead climbing, climbers will use carabiners and rope to secure themselves to the course as they climb higher and higher.

Surfing

In surfing, one of the sports making its debut this Olympics, athletes ride the waves in the open ocean and score points based on the maneuvers performed, as well as their speed, power, and flow. Each heat has four competitors and lasts for about 20 to 30 minutes. The two highest scores that the athletes receive during that time count toward their final score, and the best two athletes from the event proceed to the next one.

Table Tennis

Table tennis is similar to tennis in that the objective is the same: to hit the ball into your opponent's side of the court and have the opponent fail to return the ball after one bounce. However, as the name implies, table tennis is played on a table instead of a court. Table tennis players use different racquets and balls, too.

Table tennis also has a slightly different scoring system than tennis, and none of the complicated terminology. In table tennis, the first competitor (singles matches) or pair of competitors (doubles matches) to 11 points wins. However, similar to tennis, the winner must win by a difference of two points. This means that if the score is tied 10-10, the competitor must score two more points to win.

Tae Kwon Do

Tae kwon do is similar to the kumite (sparring) competition of karate. In tae kwon do, the goal is to score points by landed punches and kicks on your opponents, with more difficult techniques being awarded more points. The primary difference between the two is that tae kwon do focuses more heavily on kicks while karate focuses more on punching. The match system is also slightly different. Instead of three-minute matches, one tae kwon do match consists of three rounds. Each round is two minutes long, and athletes are given one-minute breaks between each round.

Tennis

A tennis court is divided into halves, one for each competitor (singles matches) or pair of competitors (doubles matches). A net divides the court in the center, and players use racquets to hit a tennis ball back and forth over the net. The goal is for the athlete to hit the ball into their opponent's side of the court and have the opponent fail to return it after one bounce.

The most confusing aspect for most people is the terminology used in the scoring system:

>> **Love:** 0 points

>> **15:** 1 point

>> **30:** 2 points

>> **40:** 3 points

>> **All:** Score is tied 15-15 or 30-30. Usually said as "15 all" or "30 all."

>> **Deuce:** Score is tied 40-40.

In general, the first athlete to score 4 points wins the game. However, the player must win by a difference of two points, which means in the event of a deuce, athletes must score two more points in order to win instead of one. If the server wins the deuce point, it's referred to as "ad-in." If the receiver wins the deuce point, it's referred to as "ad-out." If the score is ad-in and the server wins the next point, she wins the game; similarly, if the score is ad-out and the receiver wins the next point, the receiver wins the game. And finally, if the score is ad-in or ad-out, and the person with the advantage *doesn't* win the next point, the score goes back to deuce. A game can go from ad-in or ad-out to deuce many times before the game is finally won.

One match consists of three games, and the athlete to win the best two out of three games moves on to the next event.

Triathlon

Like the pentathlon, the triathlon is designed to test an athlete's overall athletic prowess. However, as opposed to the pentathlon, where athletes compete in five sports, the triathlon consists of three:

>> A 1,500-meter (0.93-mile) swim

>> A 40-kilometer (24.9-mile) cycling race

>> A 10-kilometer (6.2-mile) run

Joining the individual competitions at the Tokyo 2020 Summer Olympics will be a new mixed relay event.

Volleyball

The objective of volleyball is straightforward: to hit the ball over the net and into your opponent's side of the court and have it hit the ground before your opponent can return the ball. The ball can only be touched by a team three times before being sent back to the other team (meaning the third contact with the ball must be the one to send it over the net).

There are two different volleyball disciplines: traditional volleyball and beach volleyball.

Beach volleyball

Beach volleyball consists of teams of two players and is played on — you guessed it — a beach. One match consists of three sets, and the team to win the best two out of three sets wins the match. The first pair to score 21 points wins the set. In the event that a third set is played (each team has won one set), the third set will only be played until 15 points.

Volleyball

Traditional volleyball consists of teams of six players and is played on an indoor court. One match consists of five sets. The first four sets are won by being the first to score 25 points. The last set is won by being the first to score 15 points. However, a set must be won by a difference of 2 points. This means that if the score is tied 24-24, a team must score two more points in order to win the game. The team to win the best three out of five sets wins the match.

Weightlifting

In weightlifting, an athlete lifts a bar with weights on each end in the air over her head. The objective is simply to lift more weight than the other competitors in her weight class. However, although the objective is simple, weightlifting is anything but easy. There are two different types of lifts:

>> **Clean and jerk:** In the clean and jerk, the athlete may first lift the bar with weights from the floor up to her chest before lifting it up over her head.

>> **Snatch:** In the snatch lift, the athlete must lift the bar from the floor to above her head in one motion.

Athletes are given three attempts at each type of lift, and the highest score from each type of lift is combined to create their final score.

Wrestling

In wrestling, the athlete's goal is to pin his opponent down on the mat. However, there are two different ways a wrestling match can be won. Ideally, an athlete wants to pin his opponent with both shoulders held down for one second. This is called a *fall* and ends the match. Athletes also score points throughout the match by putting their opponents at a disadvantage. If no fall is made at the end of three minutes, the athlete with the most points scored wins.

It's also worth noting that there are two different types of events based on the two different wrestling styles:

>> **Greco-Roman:** In Greco-Roman, wrestlers can only use their upper bodies and arms.

>> **Freestyle:** In freestyle, wrestlers can use any parts of their bodies.

Chapter **7**

Budgeting for Tickets

D
epending on how many events you want to see, tickets to events can quickly become the most expensive aspect of watching the Olympics in person, possibly even more expensive than your flight or accommodations. As such, you'll want to check out the prices of the different events you're interested in before actually buying the tickets.

Ticket Categories

Tickets are divided into categories (typically labeled A though E). The categories are based on where the seats are located at the venue. For example, category A tickets are typically some of the best seats at the venue and get you up close and personal to the action. However, they're also the most expensive. Tickets in category E may not get you as close, but they're significantly cheaper.

The number of ticket categories varies by sport and venue. The opening and closing ceremonies offer six different categories for tickets (labeled A through E). Fencing, on the other hand, only has two ticket categories (labeled A and B).

Ticket Prices

Be aware that when looking at ticket prices online, you may see a couple of different numbers:

>> **Face value:** The price that the ticket is being sold for in Japan. This number is sometimes displayed in yen or the U.S. dollar equivalent.

>> **Ticket price:** Authorized Ticket Resellers (ATRs) are allowed to increase the price by up to 20 percent of the face value (more about ATRs in Chapter 9). This means that if the face value of the ticket is $106.73, ATRs can add up to $21.35 to the price of the ticket, and you can bet ATRs increase it the full 20 percent, meaning the actual price you would pay for the ticket in the United States would be $128.08.

The tables in the following sections show the different prices for tickets for each sport. The price displayed is the total amount you would pay for the ticket (including the price increase from the ATR).

Opening and closing ceremonies

The opening and closing ceremonies are likely some of the biggest events of the Olympics, and you can see that reflected in the prices (see Table 7-1). They've also been some of the hardest events to get tickets for. Both ceremonies will be held in the Olympic Stadium, which has a seating capacity of 68,000.

TABLE 7-1 Opening and Closing Ceremonies

Event	A	B	C	D	E
Opening	$2,969.15	$2,406.37	$1,096.45	$494.86	$139.73
Closing	$2,192.90	$1,775.67	$853.87	$397.83	$139.73

Aquatics

The sport of aquatics consists of five different disciplines: artistic swimming (see Table 7-2), diving (see Table 7-3), marathon swimming (see Table 7-4), swimming (see Table 7-5), and water polo (see Table 7-6). The swimming, artistic swimming, and diving events will be held at the Tokyo Aquatics Center, which has a seating capacity of 15,000. Marathon swimming will be held at Odaiba Marine Park, which has a seating capacity of 5,500. Water polo will be at the Tatsumi Water Polo Centre, which has a seating capacity of 4,700.

TABLE 7-2 **Artistic Swimming**

Event	A	B	C	D
Preliminaries	$160.68	$128.08	$81.50	$46.57
Finals	$494.86	$407.53	$203.76	$67.54

TABLE 7-3 **Diving**

Event	A	B	C	D
Preliminaries	$116.44	$93.14	$67.54	$40.75
Semifinals	$145.55	$116.44	$81.50	$58.22
Finals	$354.16	$285.28	$145.55	$93.14

TABLE 7-4 **Marathon Swimming**

Event	A	B
All events	$64.04	$40.75

TABLE 7-5 **Swimming**

Event	A	B	C	D
Preliminaries	$422.09	$349.31	$116.44	$67.54
Semifinals and finals	$1,106.15	$756.84	$412.38	$137.40

TABLE 7-6 Water Polo

Event	A	B	C
Preliminaries	$116.44	$93.14	$34.93
Quarterfinals	$145.55	$116.44	$52.39
Semifinals	$168.83	$133.91	$52.39
Finals	$209.59	$169.83	$58.22

Archery

Archery (see Table 7-7) has a total of five different types of events: women's team, men's team, mixed team, women's individual, and men's individual. All these events will be held at Yumenoshima Park Archery Field, which has a total seating capacity of 5,600.

TABLE 7-7 Archery

Event	A
Preliminaries	$34.93
Quarterfinals, semifinals, and finals	$81.50

Athletics

Athletics has three main disciplines: marathon (see Table 7-8), race walk, and track and field (see Table 7-9). However, tickets to the race walk are not for sale, so only the marathon and track-and-field events will have tickets available for purchase. The track-and-field events will be held at the Olympic Stadium, which has a seating capacity of 68,000. The marathon event was also originally scheduled to be held at the Olympic Stadium but was moved to Sapporo Odori Park (as of this writing, seating capacity information had not been released).

TABLE 7-8 Marathon

Event	A	B	C
All events	$69.86	$46.57	$29.11

TABLE 7-9 Track and Field

Event	A	B	C	D	E
Morning preliminaries	$157.19	$128.08	$110.62	$69.86	$34.93
Morning final 1	$291.10	$221.23	$168.83	$81.50	$46.57
Morning final 2	$349.31	$244.52	$186.30	$93.14	$58.22
Evening final 1	$713.18	$582.19	$349.31	$116.44	$67.54
Evening final 2	$1,319.62	$1,106.15	$460.90	$137.40	$67.54

Unlike other sports, whose tickets prices are divided into stages of the competition (preliminaries versus finals), track-and-field events are divided into five different categories: morning preliminary, morning final 1, morning final 2, evening final 1, and evening final 2. This was done to allow different pricing levels based on the popularity of some of the events being held.

Badminton

Like archery, badminton (see Table 7-10) has five different types of events: women's doubles, men's doubles, mixed doubles, women's singles, and men's singles. All badminton events will be held at Musashino Forest Sport Plaza, which has a seating capacity of 7,200.

TABLE 7-10 Badminton

Event	A	B	C	D
Preliminaries	$157.19	$128.08	$81.50	$46.57
Quarterfinals and semifinals	$244.52	$195.61	$149.04	$87.32
Semifinals and finals	$494.86	$407.53	$203.76	$93.14

Baseball and softball

The baseball events (see Table 7-11) and softball events (see Table 7-12) will be held at two different stadiums: Fukushima Azuma Baseball Stadium and Yokohama Baseball Stadium. Given that Yokohama Baseball Stadium has a seating capacity of 35,000, while Fukushima Azuma Baseball Stadium only has a seating capacity of 14,300, ticket availability may depend on which stadium the event is being held at.

TABLE 7-11 Baseball

Event	A	B	C	D
Preliminaries (Fukushima)	$157.19	$128.08	$81.50	$46.57
Preliminaries (Yokohama)	$180.48	$139.73	$93.14	$46.57
Knockout stage	$267.80	$209.59	$139.73	$69.86
Semifinals	$359.02	$279.44	$186.30	$93.14
Bronze-medal match	$494.86	$407.53	$232.87	$104.80
Finals	$713.18	$582.19	$349.31	$116.44

TABLE 7-12 Softball

Event	A	B	C	D
Preliminaries (Yokohama), one match	$93.14	$81.50	$58.22	$29.11
Preliminaries (Yokohama), two matches	$150.83	$120.67	$84.47	$42.23
Preliminaries (Fukushima)	$150.83	$120.67	$84.47	$42.23
Semifinals	$209.59	$168.83	$93.14	$46.57
Finals	$296.92	$232.87	$149.04	$87.32

Basketball

Basketball is actually split into two disciplines: basketball (the traditional basketball you see on TV; see Table 7-13) and 3x3 basketball (see Table 7-14). The regular basketball games will be held at Saitama Super Arena (with a seating capacity of 21,000), while the 3x3 basketball events will be held at Aomi Urban Sports Park (with a seating capacity of 7,100).

TABLE 7-13 Basketball

Event	A	B	C	D
Women's preliminaries	$116.44	$93.14	$58.22	$34.93
Women's quarterfinals	$209.59	$168.83	$110.62	$69.86
Women's semifinals	$296.92	$232.87	$149.04	$87.32
Women's finals	$494.86	$645.26	$460.90	$218.90
Men's preliminaries	$285.28	$203.76	$145.55	$67.54
Men's quarterfinals	$582.19	$480.30	$349.31	$116.44
Men's semifinals	$756.84	$616.15	$412.38	$137.40
Men's finals	$1,106.15	$645.26	$460.90	$218.90

TABLE 7-14 3x3 Basketball

Event	A	B	C
Preliminaries	$128.08	$93.14	$34.93
Quarterfinals	$174.66	$116.44	$58.22
Semifinals	$186.30	$139.73	$81.50
Finals	$209.59	$174.66	$104.80

Boxing

The schedule for boxing was released significantly later than the rest of the event schedule due to some conflicts with the International Boxing Association (AIBA), which was considered the "governing body" of the sport. After AIBA was suspended by the International Olympic Committee (IOC), a taskforce was put in place and the event schedule was finalized in July 2019.

Boxing events (see Table 7-15) will be held at the Kokugikan Arena, which has a seating capacity of 7,300. Like many combat sports, competitions are divided by weight class, ranging from Fly (the lightest weight class) to Super Heavy for the men, and Fly to Middle for the women.

TABLE 7-15 Boxing

Event	A	B	C	D
Preliminaries	$150.83	$118.25	$78.43	$42.23
Quarterfinals	$187.03	$144.80	$114.64	$72.40
Semifinals	$253.40	$202.72	$154.45	$90.50
Finals	$512.83	$422.33	$211.16	$96.33

Canoe

Canoeing contains two different disciplines: slalom (see Table 7-16) and sprint (see Table 7-17). The slalom discipline includes both the canoe slalom and kayak slalom events, which will be held at the Kasai Canoe Slalom Centre (with a seating capacity of 7,500). The sprint discipline includes various events, including single kayaks, double kayaks, single canoe, and double canoe, covering anywhere from 200 meters to 1,000 meters in distance. These events will be held at the Sea Forest Waterway (with a seating capacity of 12,800).

TABLE 7-16 Canoe – Slalom

Event	A	B	C
Preliminaries	$64.04	$46.57	$34.93
Semifinals and finals	$116.44	$81.50	$58.22

TABLE 7-17 Canoe – Sprint

Event	A	B	C
Preliminaries and quarterfinals	$64.04	$40.75	$34.93
Semifinals and finals	$110.62	$67.54	$58.22

Cycling

Cycling contains a total of five different disciplines. The two BMX disciplines — freestyle (see Table 7-18) and racing (see Table 7-19) — will be held at the Ariake Urban Sports Park. During the BMX racing events, the venues will have a seating capacity of 5,000, but during the BMX freestyle events, it will have a seating capacity of 6,600. The track and mountain bike disciplines will be held in Izu. The Izu Velodrome, which will be used for the track event (see Table 7-20) has a seating capacity of 3,600, while the Izu MTB Course for the mountain bike events (see Table 7-21) has a seating capacity of 11,500. Fuji International Speedway serves as the finish for the road race (see Table 7-22) and can seat 22,000.

TABLE 7-18 **BMX Freestyle**

Event	A	B
Preliminaries	$46.57	$29.11
Finals	$116.44	$58.22

TABLE 7-19 **BMX Racing**

Event	A	B
Quarterfinals	$64.04	$34.93
Semifinals and finals	$145.55	$81.50

TABLE 7-20 **Track**

Event	A	B	C
All	$168.83	$93.14	$46.57

TABLE 7-21 **Mountain Bike**

Event	A
All events	$58.22

TABLE 7-22 **Road Race**

Event	A	B
All events	$64.04	$40.75

Equestrian

The equestrian sport contains three different disciplines: dressage (see Table 7-23), eventing (see Table 7-24), and jumping (see Table 7-25). The eventing cross-country event will be held at Sea Forest Cross-Country Course, which has a seating capacity of 16,000. All other equestrian events will be held at the Equestrian Park, which can seat 9,300.

TABLE 7-23 Dressage

Event	A	B	C
Preliminaries	$75.68	$58.22	$34.93
Finals	$186.30	$128.08	$64.04

TABLE 7-24 Eventing

Event	A	B	C
Eventing dressage preliminaries	$75.68	$58.22	$34.93
Eventing cross-country preliminaries	$46.57	N/A	N/A
Eventing jumping final	$186.30	$128.08	$64.04

TABLE 7-25 Jumping

Event	A	B	C
Qualifiers	$75.68	$58.22	$34.93
Finals	$186.30	$128.08	$64.04

Fencing

All fencing events (see Table 7-26) will be held in Hall B of Makuhari Messe Hall, which has a seating capacity of 8,000. This will encompass both team and individual foil, épée, and sabre events.

TABLE 7-26 **Fencing**

Event	A	B
Preliminaries, quarterfinals, and semifinals	$87.32	$34.93
Semifinals and finals	$133.91	$75.68

Soccer

Soccer events will be held in six different venues. Which dome the event is being held in will not only affect the seating capacity (ranging from 4,800 to 72,000) and number of available tickets, but also the distance you'll have to travel in order to attend the event. You'll want to keep both of these factors in mind when purchasing tickets (see Table 7-27).

TABLE 7-27 **Soccer**

Event	A	B	C	D
Women's preliminaries, one match	$75.68	$52.39	$40.75	$29.11
Women's preliminaries, two matches	$93.14	$69.86	$46.57	$34.93
Women's quarterfinals	$180.48	$93.14	$69.86	$46.57
Women's semifinals	$244.52	$149.04	$87.32	$67.54
Women's finals	$494.86	$285.28	$145.55	$87.32
Men's preliminaries	$114.11	$75.68	$64.04	$34.93
Men's quarterfinals	$244.52	$149.04	$87.32	$67.54
Men's semifinals	$354.16	$203.76	$145.55	$87.32
Men's final	$713.18	$349.31	$174.66	$114.11

Golf

Both men's and women's golfing events (see Table 7-28), including both the preliminaries and finals, will be held at Kasumigaseki Country Club, which has a seating capacity of 25,000.

TABLE 7-28 Golf

Event	A
Preliminaries	$81.50
Finals	$116.44

Gymnastics

Gymnastics has three different disciplines: artistic (see Table 7-29), rhythmic (see Table 7-30), and trampoline (see Table 7-31). All events, including the floor routine, parallel bars, vaulting, and more will be held at the Ariake Gymnastics Centre, which will have a seating capacity of 12,000 for all disciplines and events.

TABLE 7-29 Artistic

Event	A	B	C
Qualifications	$296.92	$122.26	$46.57
Finals	$756.84	$412.38	$137.40

TABLE 7-30 Rhythmic

Event	A	B	C
Qualifications	$139.73	$110.62	$46.57
Finals	$407.53	$203.76	$67.54

TABLE 7-31 Trampoline

Event	A	B	C
All	$186.30	$128.08	$64.04

Handball

Similar to other events, handball tickets (see Table 7-32) are separated for men's and women's events, as well as the various competition stages (such as preliminaries, quarterfinals, semi-finals, and finals). All events will be held at Yoyogi National Stadium, which has a seating capacity of 10,200.

TABLE 7-32 **Handball**

Event	A	B	C
Preliminaries	$110.62	$67.54	$40.75
Quarterfinals	$116.44	$81.50	$46.57
Semifinals	$133.91	$90.82	$64.04
Bronze-medal match	$149.04	$93.14	$64.04
Finals	$232.87	$149.04	$87.32

Hockey

Both men's and women's hockey events (see Table 7-33) will be held at Oi Hockey Stadium (with a seating capacity of 15,000). Ticket prices vary based on which stage of the competition you're watching.

TABLE 7-33 **Hockey**

Event	A	B
Preliminaries	$46.57	$29.11
Quarterfinals	$87.32	$52.39
Semifinals	$110.62	$58.22
Finals	$116.44	$69.86

Judo

Judo (see Table 7-34) features a total of 15 different events — 7 for men, 7 for women, and a mixed team event. Events for men and women are separated by weight class. All 15 events will be held at Nippon Budokan, which has a seating capacity of 11,000.

TABLE 7-34 **Judo**

Event	A	B	C	D
Eliminations and quarterfinals	$180.48	$139.73	$93.14	$46.57
Semifinals and finals	$582.19	$480.30	$349.31	$116.44

Karate

Karate (see Table 7-35) is one of the new sports making its debut at the Tokyo 2020 Olympics, and, like many martial arts events, it will be held at Nippon Budokan (with a seating capacity of 11,000). It features two main events: kumite, which is divided into various weight classes, and kata.

TABLE 7-35 Karate

Event	A	B	C	D
Eliminations	$93.14	$75.68	$58.22	$40.75
Eliminations, semifinals, and finals	$149.04	$128.08	$81.50	$64.04

Modern pentathlon

The modern pentathlon (see Table 7-36) is a sport that combines five different events into one. The first is a fencing ranking round, which is held at the Musashino Forest Sport Plaza (with a seating capacity of 7,200). The other four events (swimming, fencing bonus round, riding, and laser run) will all be held at the Tokyo Stadium (with a seating capacity of 4,800).

TABLE 7-36 Modern Pentathlon

Event	A	B
Preliminary (fencing ranking)	$29.11	N/A
Final	$46.57	$29.11

Rowing

Rowing (see Table 7-37) has two main events — sculling and sweep — both of which will be held at Sea Forest Waterway (with a seating capacity of 16,000). The sculling events are further divided into single, double, and quadruple sculls, while the sweep events are divided into the pairs, fours, and eights events.

TABLE 7-37 Rowing

Event	A	B	C
Heats, quarterfinals, and semifinals	$64.04	$40.75	$34.93
Semifinals and finals	$110.62	$67.54	$58.22

Rugby

The women's rugby events will return to the Olympics after making its debut in the Rio 2016 Olympics. Both men's and women's rugby events (see Table 7-38) will be held at Tokyo Stadium, which has a seating capacity of 4,800.

TABLE 7-38 Rugby

Event	A	B	C	D
Women's preliminaries	$87.32	$58.22	$46.57	$29.11
Women's quarterfinals	$116.44	$93.14	$58.22	$40.75
Women's semifinals	$133.91	$90.82	$64.04	$46.57
Women's finals	$168.83	$110.62	$69.86	$52.39
Men's preliminaries	$116.44	$93.14	$58.22	$40.75
Men's quarterfinals	$168.83	$133.91	$75.68	$46.57
Men's semifinals	$186.30	$145.55	$81.50	$64.04
Men's finals	$296.92	$232.87	$145.55	$87.32

Sailing

Sailing (see Table 7-39) will have two new events for the Tokyo 2020 Olympics: the 49er FX Skiff for women and the Nacra 17 as a mixed event. These will be joined by traditional events such as the Laser, RS:X, 470, 49er, and Finn. All sailing events will be held at Enoshima Yacht Harbour, with a seating capacity of 3,600.

TABLE 7-39 Sailing

Event	A
Preliminaries	$34.93
Finals	$64.04

Shooting

Shooting contains two main disciplines: rifle and pistol (see Table 7-40) and shotgun (see Table 7-41). The rifle and pistol discipline contains a total of seven different events — some for men, some for women, and some for mixed teams. The events are separated by type of weapon shot and distance shot from. The shotgun discipline contains two different types of events — trap and skeet — which are also further divided into separate events for men, women, and mixed teams.

TABLE 7-40 Rifle and Pistol

Event	A
Preliminaries	$29.11
Finals	$46.57
Preliminaries and finals	$64.04

TABLE 7-41 Shotgun

Event	A
Preliminaries	$29.11
Preliminaries and finals	$46.57

All shooting events are held at the Asaka Shooting Range, but seating capacity (and, therefore, available tickets) will vary based on the event. For the rifle and pistol qualifications events, the range will only have a seating capacity of 800, but for the rifle and pistol finals, it will have a seating capacity of 2,400. The shotgun events will have a seating capacity of 3,000.

Skateboarding

Skateboarding has two different disciplines: park (see Table 7-42) and street (see Table 7-43). Events for these disciplines will be divided into men's and women's events, but all skateboarding events will be held at Ariake Urban Sports Park (with a seating capacity of 7,000).

TABLE 7-42 Park

Event	A	B
Women's events	$93.14	$46.57
Men's events	$133.91	$64.04

TABLE 7-43 Street

Event	A	B
Women's events	$93.14	$46.57
Men's events	$133.91	$64.04

Sport climbing

Sport climbing (see Table 7-44) is making its debut at the Tokyo 2020 Olympics and will be held at the Aomi Urban Sports Park (with a seating capacity of 8,400). For this sport, the different types of sport climbing have been combined into one event (instead of being separated into different events, as is typically done for other sports). This means that bouldering, lead, and speed climbing (see Chapter 6) will all be part of the competition.

TABLE 7-44 Sport Climbing

Event	A	B
Qualifications	$58.22	$34.93
Finals	$145.55	$69.86

Surfing

Surfing (see Table 7-45) is another one of the new sports making its debut at the Tokyo 2020 Olympics. It will be held in the form of an Olympic Surfing Festival, which will be held at the Tsurigasaki Surfing Beach (with a seating capacity of 6,000) instead of an artificial wave pool, so the festival has been scheduled for a total of eight days (even though it can be completed in four days) to allow for optimal wave conditions.

TABLE 7-45 Surfing

Event	A
All events	$34.93

Table tennis

Table tennis events (see Table 7-46) will be held at the Tokyo Metropolitan Gymnasium (with a seating capacity of 7,000) and will be divided into individual men's and women's events, men's and women's team events, and mixed team events.

TABLE 7-46 Table Tennis

Event	A	B	C
Preliminaries	$114.11	$75.68	$40.75
Quarterfinals	$149.04	$93.14	$64.04
Semifinals	$168.83	$110.62	$69.86
Semifinals and finals	$407.53	$203.76	$93.14

Tae kwon do

Like other martial arts sports, tae kwon do events (see Table 7-47) will be divided into men's and women's events, and further divided by weight class. All tae kwon do events will be held in Hall A of the Makuhari Messe Hall, which has a seating capacity of 10,000.

TABLE 7-47 Tae Kwon Do

Event	A	B	C
Preliminaries, quarterfinals, and semifinals	$64.04	$46.57	$34.93
Semifinals and finals	$110.62	$75.68	$58.22

Tennis

Tennis (see Table 7-48) has three different types of events: singles, doubles, and mixed doubles. All tennis events will be held at Ariake Tennis Park, which has a seating capacity of 19,900. However, note that Ariake Tennis Park has several different courts that matches will be held on, so availability of category B, C, and D tickets will depend on which court the event is being held on.

TABLE 7-48 Tennis

Event	A	B	C	D
Preliminaries	$34.93	N/A	N/A	N/A
Preliminaries and quarterfinals	$139.73	$110.62	$69.86	$46.57
Quarterfinals and semifinals	$232.87	$195.61	$149.04	$87.32
Bronze-medal match	$285.28	$203.76	$93.14	N/A
Finals	$582.19	$480.30	$349.31	$116.44

Triathlon

Although the triathlon (see Table 7-49) traditionally consisted of separate men's and women's races, the Tokyo 2020 Olympics will be introducing a new event to the sport that consists of a mixed team relay. Both the men's and women's events, as well as the mixed team events, will take place at the Odaiba Marine Park (with a seating capacity of 5,500).

TABLE 7-49 Triathlon

Event	A	B
All events	$93.14	$46.57

Volleyball

Volleyball has two different disciplines: beach volleyball (see Table 7-50) and indoor volleyball (which is known simply as volleyball; see Table 7-51). The beach volleyball events will be held at Shiokaze Park (with a seating capacity of 12,000), while the indoor volleyball events will be held at Ariake Arena (with a seating capacity of 15,000).

TABLE 7-50 Beach Volleyball

Event	A	B	C
Preliminaries	$133.91	$90.82	$40.75
Quarterfinals	$168.83	$110.62	$69.86
Semifinals	$232.87	$149.04	$87.32
Semifinals and finals	$494.86	$285.28	$93.14

TABLE 7-51 Volleyball

Event	A	B	C	D
Preliminaries	$157.19	$128.08	$81.50	$46.57
Quarterfinals	$244.52	$195.61	$149.04	$87.32
Semifinals	$354.16	$285.28	$203.76	$93.14
Finals	$582.19	$480.30	$349.31	$116.44

Weightlifting

The weightlifting events (see Table 7-52), which will be held at the Tokyo International Forum (with a seating capacity of 5,000), are not only divided into men's and women's events, but are also divided into weight class.

TABLE 7-52 Weightlifting

Event	A	B
Eliminations	$58.22	$29.11
Finals	$149.04	$81.50

Wrestling

Wrestling (see Table 7-53) has two different styles: Greco-Roman and freestyle. Events are divided based on these styles and are further divided by weight class. Freestyle events are also further divided into men's and women's events while the Greco-Roman events will be men only. All wrestling events will be held in Hall A at the Makuhari Messe Hall (with a seating capacity of 10,000).

TABLE 7-53 Wrestling

Event	A	B	C	D
Preliminaries	$157.19	$128.08	$81.50	$46.57
Finals	$494.86	$407.53	$203.76	$93.14

IN THIS CHAPTER

» Finding out about the Olympic Torch Relay

» Finding great places to watch the sports without tickets

» Discovering other ways to get involved with the Olympics

Chapter **8**

Other Olympic Activities

id you know that more goes on at the Olympics than just the different sporting events? The Olympic Games provide opportunities not just for athletes but also spectators to interact and learn more about other cultures and people. They also provide additional ways for fans to get involved with the sports.

Watching the Torch Relay

The torch not only represents the Olympic ideals of peace, unity, and friendship, but also serves as a symbol of hope. The Torch Relay is probably one of the most iconic aspects of the Olympics, aside from the sports themselves.

The torch is lit in Olympia, Greece, before being transported to the host country. It's seen as a way of connecting the ancient games to the modern games. For the Tokyo 2020 Olympics, the torch will be carried to all 47 prefectures (states) in Japan, before finally arriving in Tokyo. Before arriving in Tokyo, it will be put on display in the various areas of the Tohoku region, which were severely damaged by the earthquake and tsunami that hit in March 2011.

TIP

You can find full details of the route and schedule on the Tokyo 2020 website (https://tokyo2020.org/en/special/torch/olympic/schedule). As of this writing, exact details for the routes have not yet been finalized, but a general outline of what happens each day of the torch relay can also be found on the Tokyo 2020 website (`https://tokyo2020.org/en/special/torch/olympic/about/flow`).

Attending the TOKYO 2020 NIPPON FESTIVAL

The TOKYO 2020 NIPPON FESTIVAL will be a special festival designed to help build enthusiasm in the Olympics and will feature four different *themes* (types of events):

>> **Celebrating the Start of the Games:** The first theme will kick off in April 2020 and feature performances that fuse both Western theater (opera) and Eastern theater (kabuki). Given that one of the main focal points of the Tokyo 2020 Olympics vision is the unity of cultures, this performance will focus on the integration of both cultures.

>> **Participation, Interaction, and Dialogue:** The second theme will begin immediately prior to the opening of the Olympic Games. It will give visitors a chance to interact with and experience Japanese culture, similar to the way that athletes from all over the world will be interacting with each other during the Olympic Games.

>> **Reconstruction of the Tohoku Region:** The third theme will feature the MOCCO Giant Puppet. During the months of May, June, and July 2020, this figure will travel to various parts of the Tohoku region, the northern part of Japan, which was hit by the March 2011 tsunami and nuclear accident, and eventually make his way to Tokyo. Along the way, he'll get to meet with many different people, putting smiles on faces and encouraging more people to visit the Tohoku region.

>> **Towards the Realization of Inclusive Society:** The fourth theme will kick off in August 2020, just before the Paralympic Games. It will include performances from people coming from all sorts of different backgrounds and walks of life, including those with impairments, as well as those from the LGBTQ community. The goal is for the festival to create new friendships with those who may be different from ourselves.

As of this writing, venues and locations for the events are yet to be announced. You can find more info about the festival and events on the Tokyo 2020 Olympics website (https://tokyo2020.org/en/special/festival).

Checking Out Other Fun Attractions

Unless you got really lucky when it came to buying tickets for the different sporting events, you'll have a day or two (or several) where you won't have any events to watch. However, there are still plenty of ways to get involved in the Olympic Games even when you're not physically attending the events!

Live Sites

The Tokyo 2020 Olympics has seen an unprecedented demand for tickets. However, Live Sites will be set up around the country in order to give non-ticket-holders an opportunity to not only watch the Games, but share in the excitement with other spectators. Tokyo 2020 Live Sites will be set up by the Tokyo Organizing Committee of the Olympic and Paralympic Games, but other community Live Sites and public viewing areas will be set up by regional municipalities, educational institutions, and other organizations.

TIP

If you weren't able to get tickets to some of the events you were interested in watching, Live Sites will be a fantastic way to watch the events while sharing in the excitement.

You can find more information about Live Sites and a full list of locations on the Tokyo 2020 Olympic Games website: https://tokyo2020.org/en/get-involved/livesite.

Partner Houses

Why travel hundreds of miles to various countries when you can get a feel for all of them in one place? During the Olympics, *Partner Houses* will be set up by representatives of various countries and sports federations. Each Partner House was created to reflect the core of that country or sport, allowing visitors to experience different cultures and sports while meeting new people. Additional information about the Partner Houses can be found on the Tokyo 2020 website (https://tokyo2020.org/en/get-involved/spectators/enjoy-tokyo).

Spectaculars

Spectaculars are visual installations or Olympic icons that will be set up around the country to help build excitement for the Olympics. Some of them will be traditional Olympic logos, while others will showcase the Tokyo 2020 Olympics emblems and mascots. How many of them will you be able to find? I'll give you a hint: The basic plan can be found on the Tokyo Metropolitan Government website (www.metro.tokyo.jp/english/topics/2019/documents/0402_en.pdf).

Planning Your Trip

Chapter **9**

Buying Tickets to the Games

Tickets for the Tokyo 2020 Olympics have been in high demand. The process for buying tickets is even more complicated by the fact that it differs from country to country. Being familiar with the process and knowing what to expect can help increase your chances of securing the tickets you want.

Where to Purchase Tokyo 2020 Tickets

The process for buying tickets will be different depending on whether you're a resident of Japan or an international traveler.

For residents of Japan

Residents of Japan can purchase tickets through the official Tokyo 2020 Official Ticketing website (`https://ticket.tokyo2020.org`) or from Tokyo 2020 Official Ticket Box Offices.

If you're a resident of Japan but you're currently not in the country (maybe you're visiting family in the United States), you can still purchase tickets through the official website. However, you can't purchase tickets through the box offices until you return to Japan (because they're only located in Japan).

For overseas travelers

Outside of Japan, tickets are made available through Authorized Ticket Resellers (ATRs). These are specifically designated by the National Olympic Committee (NOC) and are the only retailers authorized to sell Olympic tickets. A full list of the ATRs for each country can be found on the Tokyo 2020 Olympic website at https://ticket.tokyo2020.org/home/atrlist.

WARNING

You should *not* buy tickets from anywhere else; otherwise, you run the risk of receiving fake tickets or being caught scalping.

For the United States, CoSport is the official ATR. All Olympic tickets for United States residents should be purchased through the CoSport website (www.cosport.com).

Ticket Sales Timeline

Like most Olympics, the Tokyo 2020 Olympics originally held a lottery for all residents of Japan interested in purchasing tickets. This lottery was held in May 2019. Due to the overwhelming demand for tickets, additional lotteries were held for those who did not win during the first lottery. As of this writing, official ticketing booths are scheduled to be set up around the city to sell any remaining tickets in Spring 2020. More information about the tickets sales schedule in Japan can be found on the Tokyo 2020 website at https://tokyo2020.org/en/games/ticket/olympic/sale.

CoSport also held its own lottery system for U.S. residents in May 2019. Anytime during the month, those interested in entering the lottery could visit the website and select which tickets they would like to purchase. Participants of the lottery were notified of the results at the end of June and had approximately a week to purchase any of the tickets they were awarded during the lottery.

After the CoSport lottery was completed, "live sales" began on the CoSport website. This meant that any tickets not purchased during the CoSport lottery phase would be available for sale on a first-come, first-served basis. In the United States, live ticket sales began July 9, 2019; it will continue all the way through the end of the Olympics in 2020.

Purchasing Tickets from CoSport

According to an email from CoSport, interest in Tokyo 2020 Olympics event tickets has been record breaking. As such, tickets have been hard to come by, but not impossible. Available tickets can be purchased through the CoSport website. To buy tickets, follow these steps:

1. **Go to** www.cosport.com.

2. **Click Login.**

3. **Click Create an Account.**

4. **Fill in the requested information and click Submit.**

5. **Open the email from CoSport and click the link to verify your account.**

6. **Log in with your email address and password.**

7. **Hover your mouse over Tickets.**

   You see two options: Tokyo 2020 Olympic Games and Tokyo 2020 Paralympic Games (see Figure 9-1).

FIGURE 9-1: The CoSport website allows you to buy tickets to both the Olympic Games and the Paralympic Games.

8. **Click Tokyo 2020 Olympic Games.**

   The Tickets page appears.

9. **Click the Exclude Sold Out check box to hide the sold-out events (see Figure 9-2).**

WARNING

When you click the Exclude Sold Out check box, be prepared for the screen to be blank. Demand for tickets has been unprecedented. Tickets that were available when live sales began sold out almost instantly.

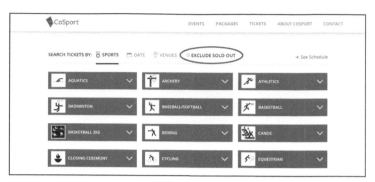

FIGURE 9-2: Click the Exclude Sold Out check box to see only the events with tickets available.

Since then, additional tickets have become available seemingly at random. This often happens as sponsors and other officials notify the Olympic Committees that they won't be attending, and tickets that had been reserved for them become available to the general public for sale.

If you're interested in purchasing tickets, your best bet is to frequently check the CoSport website — they typically don't announce when new tickets have become available, so you just have to check back over and over and over.

TIP

Alternatively, a popular website, OS Site Tracker (`www.os-site-tracker.com/en`), is allowing members to get notifications as soon as it detects that new tickets have been made available for sale on the CoSport website. If paying by PayPal, membership costs a one-time fee of $17.18.

TIP

Signing up for the CoSport newsletter is also a fantastic way of staying up to date with the latest news around ticket sales. Finally, Facebook groups created specifically to help those planning their trip to the Olympics will also often post if they see that more tickets have become available.

CoSport also offers various travel packages for the Olympics that include accommodations, as well as event tickets. To purchase a travel package, follow these steps:

1. Follow steps 1 through 7 in the previous list to create a CoSport account.

2. Hover your mouse over Tickets.

You see two options: Tokyo 2020 Olympic Games and Tokyo 2020 Paralympic Games (see Figure 9-3).

FIGURE 9-3: The CoSport website allows you to buy ticket packages for both the Olympic Games and the Paralympic Games.

3. Click Tokyo 2020 Olympic Games.

The Packages page appears listing the different package tiers (see Figure 9-4).

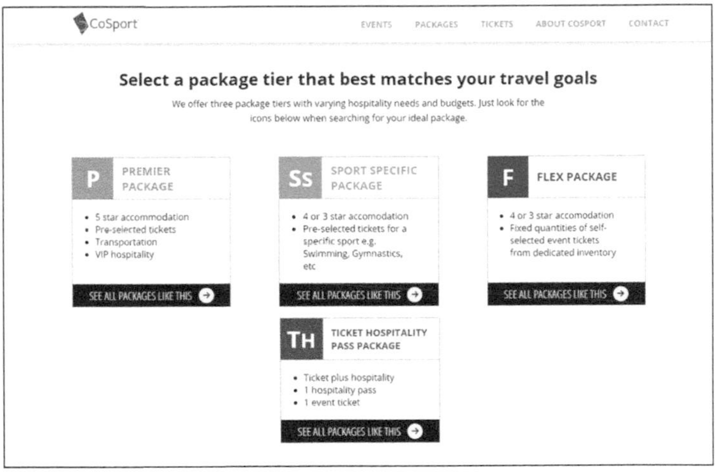

![The CoSport package tiers page showing Premier Package, Sport Specific Package, Flex Package, and Ticket Hospitality Pass Package]

FIGURE 9-4: As of this writing, CoSport offers four different package tiers.

4. Click a package tier.

A list of packages available is displayed (see Figure 9-5).

5. Select a package.

Full details of the selected package appear, including what is included in the package and a high-level itinerary.

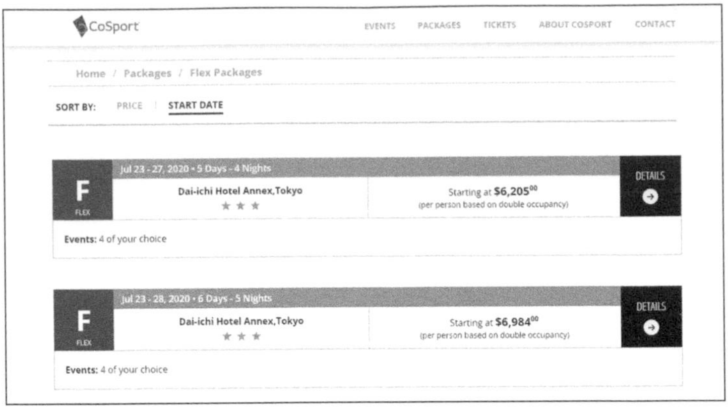

FIGURE 9-5: Each package tier offers multiple package options differing by dates and accommodation location.

6. **Scroll down to the How to Buy section (see Figure 9-6) and select the number of people staying in the accommodation and the number of packages you would like to purchase.**

   The total price based on options selected is displayed.

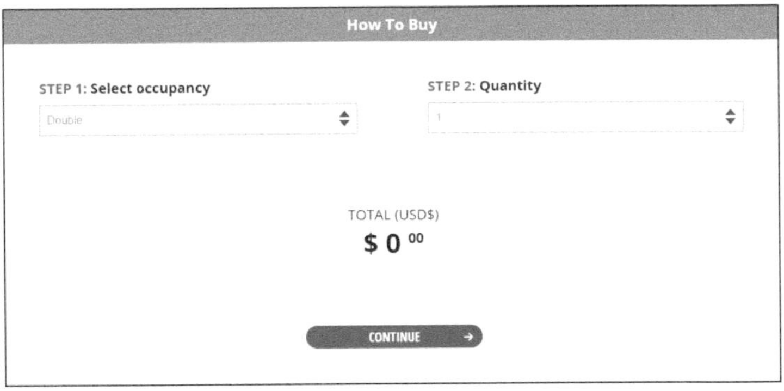

FIGURE 9-6: Changing the number of people staying in the hotel room and the quantity of ticket packages desired will change the total price.

7. **Click Continue.**

8. **Select which events you would like tickets for on each of the days of the itinerary (see Figure 9-7).**

Pick your events for the Flex package:
5 Days / 4 Nights (Jul 23 - 27, 2020)
Package Code: CSF13-DA-23

CONFIRM SELECTION →

With this Flex Package you are entitled to select events for 5 days. Please make your choices from the list below. Note that all of your selections will include 4 events to each session.

Event Selection(s)   Number of events in this package: 4 | Your selection: 4

DAY 1	Thursday 7/23/2020	1 event selected	→ Change selection	VIEW ⌄
DAY 2	Friday 7/24/2020	0 event selected		PICK EVENTS
DAY 3	Saturday 7/25/2020	1 event selected	→ Change selection	VIEW ⌄
DAY 4	Sunday 7/26/2020	1 event selected	→ Change selection	VIEW ⌄
DAY 5	Monday 7/27/2020	1 event selected	→ Change selection	VIEW ⌄

FIGURE 9-7: For each day of the itinerary, you can select a desired event from a list of available events for that day. The number of events you're able to select varies by package.

9. Click Confirm Selection.

10. Review the details to make sure all the information is correct.

11. Click Proceed to Checkout.

If you're dead-set on attending the Olympics but you can't buy individual tickets or find accommodations (see Chapter 10), you may find these packages to be a great alternative. However, be prepared for the fact that a hefty price tag comes attached to each of them. The cheapest package is $6,160 per person (assuming double occupancy in the hotel) and includes five days and four nights at a 4-star hotel, as well as four event tickets.

Chapter **10**

Traveling to Japan and Finding a Place to Stay

Often, booking flights and accommodations is the most stressful aspect of planning a trip. If this process weren't already stressful enough, it's made more complex by the fact that it's the Olympics. Some of the general rules of thumb don't apply here, so even frequent travelers who know what to expect can be thrown off.

Thankfully, with enough research and patience, getting to Japan and finding a place to stay don't have to be as intimidating as they seem.

Getting to Japan

Compared to other parts of the Tokyo 2020 Olympics trip-planning process, booking flights to Japan should be relatively easy. With a little bit of knowledge of flight options and prices, you'll be well on your way to finalizing details for your trip to Japan.

Identifying the airports in Japan

There are two main airports that travelers use when visiting the Tokyo area: Narita International Airport (NRT) and Haneda Airport (HND).

Honestly, you can't go wrong with either airport. Haneda is closer to central Tokyo, but Narita offers more international flight options. I'd go with whichever one is cheapest. Thankfully, if you type **Tokyo** into most flight search websites, you'll be given the option to choose all Tokyo airports, which will include both Haneda and Narita.

Knowing how to book flights

Several websites allow you to search for flights. However, it's important to note that not all airlines make their prices available through third-party websites. As such, I recommend using third-party sites to get an idea of prices. Then check the websites of individual airlines to see how their prices compare.

Popular and reputable third-party websites for booking flights include the following:

>> **CheapOair:** www.cheapoair.com

>> **Expedia:** www.expedia.com

>> **Google Flights:** www.google.com/flights

>> **Hotwire:** www.hotwire.com

>> **Kayak:** www.kayak.com

>> **Orbitz:** www.orbitz.com

>> **Travelocity:** www.travelocity.com

>> **TripAdvisor:** www.tripadvisor.com

TIP

I also recommend looking at multiple airports around your home, not just the closest one. You could also consider flying into one of the other major airports in Japan (such as Kansai International Airport).

For example, at one point a round-trip flight on United Airlines from Detroit to Tokyo cost $2,015 for economy class. At the same time, a flight on United Airlines from Chicago to Tokyo cost $1,350 for economy class. In this case, a four-and-a-half-hour drive could save you $665 per person. Assuming you could get the flight times to line up correctly, even adding a round-trip flight between Detroit and Chicago would only cost an additional $221, still saving you $444 per person.

Deciding when to book flights

If you haven't started looking at flights yet, I'd at least start taking a peek. When flights first started becoming available for the weeks of the Olympics in July 2019, flight prices were significantly high — approximately two to three times the normal price. However, in the following months, many airfares dropped down closer to normal prices.

But what is "normal"? This will vary greatly depending on what airport you depart from and what airport you fly into. In order to determine what would be a "normal" price for your trip, I recommend looking at flights for the same length of time departing on the same days of the week, just in different months.

For example, if you plan on attending the Olympics in its entirety, you would likely leave for Japan on Wednesday, July 22, 2020, and return on Monday, August 10, 2020, for a total of 20 days. To see how the price of this flight compared to "normal," you could look at flights from Wednesday, June 10, 2020, to Monday, June 29, 2020.

TIP

Many websites allow you to track flight prices and get notifications when prices drop. If you have enough time, I suggest watching the price of your flight for a few days or even weeks to see how the price fluctuates.

The CheapOair 2019 Annual Airfare Study looked at 917 million airfares and how their prices changed over time in order to determine the best time to purchase flights. According to the study, the "prime booking window" is between three weeks to four months prior to your trip. Flights booked more than 4 months in advance were an average of $50 more expensive.

However, this study looked at all sorts of different flights, meaning the results of this study may not necessarily ring true for flights to Tokyo during the Olympics. I'd keep the aforementioned information in mind, but if a flight you're watching drops significantly in price, it may be worth going ahead and booking the flight, even if it's outside of the prime booking window.

TIP

Also, before booking your flight, make sure to take a look at the refund and cancellation policy. If you book your flight and the price does end up dropping significantly at a later date, it may be worth canceling the flight you bought and booking the cheaper one. Many airlines have strict cancellation and refund policies, often charging a fee of $200 or more for cancellations. However, if the flight price drops by $300 or more (which it very well could), it may be worth eating the $200 fee.

Putting a Roof over Your Head

Securing tickets to the various Olympic events will likely be one of the most difficult tasks in preparation for attending the Olympics. Finding a place to stay will likely be the second-most difficult. However, if you know what to expect and look for, it likely won't be as difficult as it first may seem.

Types of accommodations

In Japan, there are many different options for the various types of travelers. There are your typical hotels, but also hostels, short-term rentals, home stays, and even capsule hotels.

Which type of accommodation is best will very much depend on what type of traveler you are. Will you be traveling with family? Do you mind sharing a shower with other guests? All these factors come into play when trying to decide what type of accommodation to book.

TIP

My recommendation is to keep your options open as much as possible. Many hotels, hostels, and Airbnbs are charging at least double what they normally charge per night and don't offer free cancellation. Keeping an open mind will help you find the best deals, even if it means staying in an Airbnb when you usually stay in a hotel.

Capsule hotels

This type of accommodation originated in Japan in the late 1970s and has begun expanding to other parts of the globe. As you may be able to guess by the name, you typically get a capsule (also known as a pod) to sleep in instead of a room. Often, one room can have dozens of capsules.

Capsule hotels originally catered to low-budget solo travelers, particularly businessmen. However, they've also become increasingly popular with women and tourists. Some capsule hotels are men only, but there are also many capsule hotels that allow both male and female guests. However, the ones that do are usually segregated so that men and women stay in different sections or on different floors.

TIP

If you decide to stay in a capsule hotel, make sure to confirm with the hotel that you can stay there before making a reservation. Not all booking websites list whether a capsule hotel is male only. I learned that one the hard way when I showed up at a capsule hotel where I'd made a reservation. A frantic desk clerk rushed up to me to quickly inform me that it was a male-only hotel and I would need to cancel my reservation.

Although staying in a capsule hotel is a unique experience, I wouldn't recommend staying in one when planning a trip to the Olympics unless you're a solo traveler who doesn't mind living out of a bookbag for the duration of your trip.

A standard capsule is almost 4 feet (1.2 meters) wide, 6.5 feet (2 meters) long, and 3.2 feet (1 meter) high. The capsules often have a light, shelves, power outlets, and a TV built in, plus curtains to close for privacy. Because the capsules aren't large enough to store many personal items, there are usually lockers in the washrooms where you can store your belongings such as a bookbag. Along with shared facilities such as bathrooms and laundry rooms, there are also typically common areas and entertainment rooms where guests can lounge.

Overall, capsule hotels are ideal if you're a minimalist traveler or you just want somewhere cheap to crash for a couple nights. However, if you plan on visiting Japan for the full duration of the Olympics, you may want something with a bit more space and comfort.

It's also worth mentioning that some capsule hotels are closer to hostels than the typical capsule-style lodging. Instead of several capsules lining a wall, a room may be sectioned off into square areas that make up the guest rooms. These rooms are often sectioned off by a sliding door and may have additional furniture, such as a desk. In general, these fancier capsule hotels aren't much more expensive and may be ideal for longer stays, but they're still typically separated by gender and provide small storage lockers (because the sliding doors to the room don't lock).

Hostels

Hostels in Japan are quite common, especially in the bigger cities. Like capsule hotels, hostels are designed for those looking for low-budget accommodations. Unlike standard hotels, they have fewer amenities such as coffee machines or hair dryers, but they're also quite a bit cheaper than hotels while still providing a decent amount of comfort.

Rooms at hostels are typically dorm style, containing several bunk beds that can accommodate four to eight people. However, for a premium rate, you can also find private rooms.

Hostels are often great for solo travelers and families traveling on a budget. You'll typically find that guests are more social at hostels than they are at capsules hotels, hanging out in common rooms like the living room or dining room.

TIP

Overall, hostels are a great option for those who are looking for a budget-friendly place to stay, particularly those who are traveling by themselves or in a group and on a tight budget.

Short-term rentals and home stays

For most people, the first thing that comes to mind for short-term rentals or home stays is Airbnb (www.airbnb.com). With Airbnb, you can rent rooms or even entire houses for the duration of your time in Japan.

The benefit of an Airbnb as opposed to a hotel is that you often get cheaper prices than the local hotels, especially if you're part of a large group. Depending on what kind of rental you get, you may even have a full kitchen and living room to relax in. The downside is that it doesn't have the 24/7 staff that a hotel would. There's no cleaning staff to come in and tidy up your room every day and no front-desk staff to ask any of the random questions that may pop into your head.

WARNING

In June 2018, Japan passed a law that all Airbnb hosts must register their listing with the government and display their registration number. Make sure the Airbnb you're considering is licensed, or you risk your reservation being canceled at the last minute.

TIP

Alternatively, if you want more of a like-a-local experience while in Japan, you could consider a home stay instead of a rental. Websites like Homestay.com (www.homestay.com) allow you to stay with a host family, allowing you to meet some of the locals and experience life in Japan firsthand. It's a great alternative if you don't mind staying with other people.

Hotels

Hotels in Japan are similar to what you would expect from hotels anywhere else you would go. They vary in class (from 1 star to 5 stars) and offer many of the typical amenities such as microwaves, coffee machines, housekeeping, and more. Plus, they're often located right by the various Olympic venues or are within walking distance of a bus stop or train station.

Ryokan

Ryokan are traditional Japanese style inns. For tourists, one of the biggest draws of ryokan is that it not only offers a place to sleep, but also offers the opportunity to experience Japanese lifestyle firsthand. They typically feature tatami floors, futon beds, and *onsen* (Japanese hot springs). Like hotels, ryokan vary from budget friendly to luxurious and are a great option for larger groups and families.

WARNING

Be aware that many ryokan charge per person (instead of per room) due to the fact that reservations typically include dinner and breakfast featuring local cuisine.

Where to stay

Hotel availability changes constantly as the Olympics get closer. The chances of my favorite hotels in Tokyo having availability at the same time you're reading this is pretty slim. Instead of focusing on the best *places* to stay during the Olympics, I'll focus on the best *areas* to stay.

One of the best things about Japan in general, and Tokyo in particular, is that it has a very extensive public transportation system. This means that you could stay out of downtown and still be able to get to the various Olympic venues without too many issues.

The two top areas to stay in for the Olympics are Shibuya and Shinjuku. These are the two largest shopping and entertainment districts in Tokyo. They're also located close to many of the Olympic venues in the Heritage Zone. Many different railway lines run through both Shinjuku Station and Shibuya Station, meaning that these stations provide quick and easy access to anywhere else you want to go. However, because Shibuya and Shinjuku are so popular, it will also likely be rough to find available accommodations in these areas. The ones that are available will likely be ridiculously expensive.

The Koto area is home to most of the Olympic venues in the Tokyo Bay Zone, making it another great option for accommodations. Staying here will allow you to be close to a significant number of the venues. However, for that same reason, accommodation availability will also be hard to come by.

Other wards or "special cities" within the Heritage Zone and or Tokyo Bay Zone include Bunkyo, Chiyoda, Chuo, Meguro, Minato, Shinagawa, Sumida, Taito, and Toshima. Any of these areas would make for great places to stay. All of them have decent-size train stations, allowing for easy access to other parts of Tokyo, and plenty of things to do.

For those who have a tight budget and don't mind a longer commute, it may be worth looking at accommodations outside of Tokyo. Some foreigners traveling to Japan are choosing to stay in Chiba or Yokohama, both of which are about an hour outside of central Tokyo by train on a normal day. During the Olympics, the commute will likely be even longer than an hour. However, for some people, the commute is worth the money saved on accommodations.

How to make reservations

If you really want to get the best deal (or any deal), this part is going to take some work. Many different websites can be used for making lodging reservations, and I suggest checking all of them. Yes, *all* of them.

TIP

Unfortunately, not all hotels, hostels, and rentals are listed on all booking websites. This means that a hotel that has availability may show up on one booking site, but not the other. If you only look at one booking website, you may be missing out on hotel availability.

Popular and reputable booking websites include the following:

>> **Agoda:** www.agoda.com

>> **Airbnb:** www.airbnb.com

>> **Booking.com:** www.booking.com

>> **Expedia:** www.expedia.com

>> **Homestay.com:** www.homestay.com

>> **Hotels.com:** www.hotels.com

>> **Kayak:** www.kayak.com

>> **Priceline:** www.priceline.com

>> **TripAdvisor:** www.tripadvisor.com

>> **Trivago:** www.trivago.com

TIP

Also make sure to check the websites of the individual hotels. Many times hotels will run their own promotional deals that aren't offered through third-party booking websites.

When to book a place to stay

Book now. Like, right now. As in, stop reading and go start looking for places to stay immediately.

Hotels, hostels, and the like typically start accepting bookings up to a year in advance. Places like Airbnbs sometimes start accepting reservations even earlier than that. This means that most places started accepting reservations back in July 2019. Given the record-breaking demand for Olympics tickets, accommodations have also been in short supply. If you haven't booked your accommodations yet, start looking.

Does this mean that you have zero chance of booking a place to stay? Not necessarily. It just depends on how patient and determined you are, as well as what you're willing to pay.

However, don't just book the first place you find that has availability.

WARNING

Prices for accommodations during the Tokyo 2020 Olympics have been anywhere from two to ten times their normal nightly rates. For example, at one point, APA Hotel Akihabaraeki Denkigaiguchi, located in Tokyo's Chiyoda District a little under two miles from the Tokyo International Forum (one of the Olympic venues) was charging $1,066 for the night of Friday, July 31, 2020. That's $1,066 for one night at a 3-star hotel with a double bed. You can book the exact same room at the exact same hotel for the night of Friday, June 12, 2020, (a little over a month before the Olympics) for $67 a night.

However, don't be discouraged by these prices. Some travelers have reported being able to score reservations at normal prices at various places around Tokyo. It just requires a bit of patience and perseverance, and a lot of luck. Other travelers have been content to book if they can find an accommodation that is no more than two and a half times the normal price. It all comes down to what you can afford.

If you can't find anything that is available within your price range right now, you have two options:

>> Wait to see if availability opens up.

>> Consider hotel jumping.

Many hotels partnered with the International Olympic Committee and blocked out rooms for sponsors and travel packages. As sponsors begin to notify the Olympic Committee that they won't be in attendance, those rooms begin to open up for the general public. The same goes for rooms that were reserved for part of travel packages. As we get closer and closer to the Olympics, if travel packages don't sell, the rooms tied up in those packages will be released for individual reservations.

The other option is simply not to stay in the same place for the entire duration of your trip. Many travelers, especially those going to the Olympics for more than just a few days, have found it significantly difficult to find availability at a hotel for the entire duration of their trip. However, you may find a hotel that has availability for a portion of your travel dates. In this case, you could book the hotel for what availability it does have and look for another hotel to stay in for the rest of your trip.

Chapter **11**

Finding Other Things to Do in Tokyo

O f course, the main reason you're going to Japan is proba-bly to watch the Olympics, but that doesn't mean you can't explore Tokyo while you're there!

Tokyo is the largest metropolitan area in the world. To help you tackle it, I've divided the city into districts. In this chapter, you find all the coolest things to do in the different parks of Tokyo.

Harajuku: The Heart of Trendy Youth Culture and Fashion

Probably one of the most famous attractions in the Harajuku area is Takeshita-dori, a street full of stores and restaurants. As you exit the Harajuku train station, you'll find yourself standing before a large entryway that reads Takeshita Street. As you walk down the most likely very crowded street, you'll find all sorts of boutiques, as well as cafes selling tasty sweets. As you walk down the street, you'll quickly find that most of the shops are geared toward teenagers. However, even if teen fashion isn't exactly your scene, it's still worth checking out, especially on the weekends, if you're into people watching. If you're lucky, you may even get to see teens and young adults dressed up in all sorts of crazy fashion outfits.

Right next door to Takeshita Street is Omotesando, another shopping street, but this one is geared more toward adults. You'll be able to recognize this street as soon as you reach it by all the massive trees that line it. As you walk down, you'll find yourself passing countless high-end fashion stores, such as Louis Vuitton, Prada, Dior, and more. You'll also come across Omotesando Hills, a shopping plaza full of even more fashion stores, restaurants, boutiques, cafes, and more.

Another thing you'll come across in Japan are 100 yen shops. These would be the equivalent of dollar stores in the United States. Specifically in Harajuku, you'll find Daiso, one of the largest 100 yen shops in Japan. It has all sorts of little knickknacks that make for great souvenirs, such as sushi erasers, decorative fans, and more. I stopped here when looking for envelopes and stationary for writing letters to friends and family back home, because I could find unique Japanese patterns instead of using plain computer paper.

TIP

If Daiso doesn't have what you're looking for in terms of souvenirs, I recommend heading over to the Oriental Bazaar (conveniently located on Omotesando Street). With its red and green building color resembling traditional Japanese architecture, you won't miss it. It's one of the largest souvenir stores in Harajuku, selling everything from T-shirts and books to larger items, such as *kimono* (traditional Japanese clothing), screens, samurai equipment, furniture, and other similar items.

Also, have you ever heard of NHK? It's Japan's national broadcasting organization. Unless you pay close attention to world news and politics, you may not have heard of it. However, for those who know of it or who are generally interested in TV and radio broadcasting, NHK Studio Park gives visitors the opportunity to get a behind-the-scenes look at the studio.

Ikebukuro: The Up-and-Coming Area

Many locals often divide Ikebukuro in half, referring to the areas as Nishi-Ikebukuro (West Ikebukuro) and Higashi-Ikebukuro (East Ikebukuro). Nishi-Ikebukuro is more of the business district (which isn't overly exciting), but it's also home to Rikkyo University. The campus is quite a bit smaller than you would expect in comparison to some of the larger universities in the United States, but it's full of greenery despite being in the middle of a large city. The main building just inside the entrance gate is also typically covered in ivy during the summer months, making it look quite prestigious.

In Higashi-Ikebukuro, you find Sunshine City, which is sort of a "city within a city." Here, you find a little bit of everything, including restaurants, shops, a planetarium, an aquarium, indoor theme parks, and an observatory.

TIP

If you don't do anything else in Sunshine City, I recommend checking out the observatory. SKY CIRCUS Sunshine 60 Observatory offers not only great views, but also other sorts of entertainment such as a virtual reality (VR) experience, a mirror maze, and more.

Also in Sunshine City is Pokémon Center Mega Tokyo. If you're a fan of the Pokémon games or TV series, you'll definitely want to make a stop here. You'll find Pokémon-themed snacks, keychains, phone cases, tableware, stationary, apparel, plush toys, and of course, trading cards.

If you have some time to kill, Round1 Entertainment is a fantastic place to hang out. The main features include bowling, arcade games, and karaoke. If you decide to give bowling a try, you'll find that Round1 offers a unique event called the Moonlight Strike Game. Typically once per hour, they stop open bowling and hold the Moonlight Strike Game. During this event, everybody bowls at once. If men manage to get a strike or women get nine pins or more, they win a prize, which is a souvenir photo.

In the arcade section of Round1, you'll find popular Japanese arcade games such as Taiko-no-Tatsujin (often called Taiko Master in English), as well as other popular games such as air hockey. Also in the arcade section is where you'll find *purikura*, Japan's fancy photo booth (see Chapter 19).

To most people in the United States, karaoke is typically associated with singing in front of other people at a bar. However, karaoke works a bit differently in Japan. Instead, you typically rent a room with friends, meaning the only people you have to worry about hearing you sing are your friends, not a bunch of strangers (although, if your friends are anything like mine, they may give you a harder time than strangers at a bar would!). And don't worry, even Japanese karaoke offers plenty of popular English songs for you to choose from!

Also in the area is SEGA Ikebukuro Gigo, a large game center owned by Sega (a large video game publisher). Inside, you'll find countless arcade games, including a floor entirely devoted to crane games, as well as an anime-themed cafe and merchandise for sale.

Across the street from SEGA is Tokyu Hands, one of the large department stores. It started as a DIY store, and you see evidence of this inside with its large supply of arts-and-crafts materials. However, it also has a wide variety of other products such as household decor, toiletries, and more. Many of the products are unique to Japan, which makes it a great place to pick up some cool stuff to make your friends and family back home jealous.

Shinjuku: The Entertainment District

Shinjuku is home to the largest train station in the world. There are many reasons for this, but one is the fact that there is just so much to do in Shinjuku. Anytime my friends and I were looking for something to do for the evening or weekend, we often found ourselves in Shinjuku.

Those who are interested in the food scene in Japan will want to stop by Omoide Yokocho. It's a very narrow alley just a few minutes from the station, but it's full of small bars and restaurants. Most of them are pretty small, having just a few barstools out front for guests, but that's part of its charm. Many of the buildings were built during the Showa-era (post–World War II) and still have their original appearance. Omoide Yokocho actually translates to "Memory Lane," and you'll definitely feel like you've stepped back in time as you stroll down this quaint alley.

One of my absolute favorite places to go in Shinjuku is Shinjuku-gyoen, also referred to as Shinjuku Garden. From the 1600s to the mid-1800s, it was actually the home of a feudal lord before being transferred to the Imperial Family and eventually opened as a public park. It costs a few yen to enter, but the walking paths through a traditional Japanese landscape garden,

French garden, and traditional English landscape garden make for a great escape when you need to get away from the hustle and bustle of the city.

Shinjuku is also home to the popular Robot Restaurant, a not-so-normal dinner theater. It's known for its very unique show including mechanical robots, dinosaurs, ninjas, dancers, and anything else you can think of. Plus, there are so many colors and lights, it's impossible to take it all in. It's definitely one of those only-in-Japan types of experiences.

Another really good spot to visit in Shinjuku is the Tokyo Metropolitan Government Building. It's in the business part of Shinjuku, away from a lot of the shopping and restaurants, so you likely wouldn't stumble upon it if you were just out and about. However, you'll know it as soon as you see it by the two large towers that extend up on either side of the building. It's worth the detour for what's at the very top of the two towers — a free observatory. At 202 meters (663 feet) high, the observatory is only one-third of the height of Tokyo Skytree in Sumida (see Chapter 19), but unlike Tokyo Skytree, it's completely free to enter.

Hidden behind some of the taller buildings in Shinjuku is Hanazono Jinja (Hanazono Shrine). Like Shinjuku-gyoen, it offers a quiet sanctuary for those looking to get away from the hustle and bustle of the city. On Sundays, it hosts a flea market full of vendors selling antiques and trinkets.

Also, don't forget to check out the Shinjuku train station itself. It's annoyingly easy to get lost in this massive train station, but sometimes those mishaps lead to the best adventures!

Shibuya: Home of Shopping and Fashion

One of the top attractions in Shibuya, and also one of the top ten things to do in Tokyo, is Meiji Jingu. Together with Yoyogi Park, its makes up a large forest area located right in the middle of the city! Within this forest, you'll find the shrine dedicated to Emperor Meiji, the first emperor of modern Japan, and his wife. Also in the area is Meiji Jingu Museum, which contains treasures from the shrine's collection, as well as artifacts that belonged to the emperor. For more information about Meiji Jingu, see Chapter 19.

Downtown you'll find the famous Shibuya Crossing, also referred to as the Shibuya Scramble. It's the world's busiest pedestrian crossing, with approximately 2,500 people crossing at once in all different directions. You can find more information and tips for visiting Shibuya Crossing in Chapter 19.

If you're looking to do some shopping, Shibuya is definitely the place to be. Women will want to check out Shibuya 109. It has nine floors full of various stores selling women's clothing and accessories! 109 Men's was originally the men's version of Shibuya 109, but it was recently renovated and reopened as Magnet by Shibuya 109. It offers not only men's apparel but also a food court and a viewing deck where you can get good views of the Shibuya Scramble.

TIP

Another good place to get a good view of the Shibuya Scramble is the newly opened Shibuya Scramble Square. Unlike many of the other large shopping complexes in the area, 33 of the businesses (out of the 39 total) are food related, making it a fantastic place to go if you absolutely love food or just aren't sure what you're in the mood to eat.

If you're interested in shopping for souvenirs as opposed to apparel, I recommend stopping by Don Quijote. This large discount store sells all sorts of Japanese souvenirs, such as keychains, hats, fans, and more. It's a great place to pick up some unique, only-in-Japan types of items for a good price!

While exploring the Shibuya Scramble area, you'll likely stumble across a statue of a dog. Those who don't know the story may find it to be a bit random, but others will know that this statue is for Hachiko, Japan's famous pooch. Legend has it that he would wait at the train station for his master to come home, and he continued to wait there even after his master passed away.

Chuo, Chiyoda, and Minato: The Center of Tokyo

Central Tokyo has long been home to the political and economic powerhouses. Here you'll find not only the imperial palace but also the world's largest fish market and one of Tokyo's premier shopping districts.

The Imperial Palace in Chiyoda is located on the former site of Edo Castle and is the home of Japan's Imperial Family. The inner grounds of the palace are not typically open to the public except for a select few days throughout the year (such as certain holidays), but the Imperial Palace East Gardens are open to the public most days of the year.

Chuo is also home to the Tsukuji Outer Market. It used to be the Tsukuji Fish Market, which contained both an outer market and an inner market. However, the inner market recently moved to Toyosu (just outside of Chuo) and was renamed to Toyosu Market. If you're a big seafood lover, both markets are definitely worth visiting. For more info on Tsukuji Outer Market and Toyosu Market, see Chapter 19.

Also in Chuo is the Ginza area, home to Tokyo's most famous upmarket shopping. It's also home to some of Japan's most expensive real estate, as well as the famous $10 cup of coffee. There aren't too many name-brand designers you won't find in this area.

Like Ikebekuro, Chuo also has a Pokémon merchandise store, but unique to the store in Chuo is a Pokémon Café. Here, you can enjoy snacks and treats surrounded by your favorite Pokémon characters — and, of course, all the food is Pokémon themed, too!

Last but not least is Tokyo Tower, located in Minato. It's based off of the Eiffel Tower in Paris, except for one major difference: It's bright red. Ironically, it's actually 13 meters (42 feet) taller than the Eiffel Tower, making it the world's tallest, self-supported steel tower. Here you'll find two observation decks, as well as a nice souvenir shop.

Asakusa: Historical Tokyo

If you're looking to delve into the traditional culture and history of Japan, you'll want to head to Asakusa.

Probably the most iconic attraction here is Senso-ji Temple, Tokyo's oldest temple. It's most recognizable for its two large gates, which have large paper lanterns and guardian statues. Inside, you'll find the main hall, as well as a large five-story pagoda. See Chapter 19 for more information on Senso-ji.

Just outside Senso-ji is Nakamise-dori, a long street full of vendors selling food and souvenirs. It's a good place to go if you're looking for unique, hard-to-find souvenirs. I found many of my Japanese wall scrolls here.

WARNING

If you're just looking for small trinket-like souvenirs, I recommend holding off and buying them at places like Daiso or Don Quijote, as you'll likely be able to find them much cheaper than you would at Nakamise-dori. However, even if you don't plan on buying souvenirs here, it's cool just to window-shop and walk past all the vendors.

Right next to Senso-ji is the Asakusa Culture Tourist Information Center. With its distinct design of sloping roofs and wooden slats, it's pretty hard to miss. It primarily features conference rooms and exhibition spaces, but it also offers a tourist information desk with staff fluent in multiple languages (including English). On the seventh floor, you'll find a cafe, and at the very top you'll find a free observation deck. It's not as high as some of the other observatories in the area, but it affords a great view of the nearby city below, including Senso-ji and Nakamise-dori.

Given that you're in Japan for the Olympics, you may not have much time to visit other parts of Japan. However, that doesn't mean you still can't appreciate everything it has to offer! Marugoto Nippon shopping center is full of souvenirs, handcrafted items, and restaurants that showcase local specialties from all over Japan. It's a fantastic way to tour the country without actually touring the country.

Drums seem to have a special place in the hearts of Japanese — they're often used in religious ceremonies, festivals, and theater performances. *Taiko,* the art of Japanese drumming, is quite popular and is sometimes a performance in itself. I highly recommend catching a taiko performance if you can while in Japan. However, even if you can't catch a show, I recommend stopping by Taikokan Drum Museum. Not only is it the world's first museum dedicated to the subject of drums, but many of the instruments on display can actually be played (which is a bit counterintuitive for most museum goers).

If you're in Asakusa but you plan on visiting other main areas in Tokyo, such as Chuo (see the preceding section), you may want to consider taking a boat rather than the usual train. Tokyo Cruise operates three unique boats: the *Himiko,* the *Hotaluna,* and the *Emeraldas*. *Himiko* is a futuristic, spaceship-looking boat that was designed by the famous comic artist Leiji Matsumoto. Both the *Hotaluna* and *Emeraldas* are sister boats to the *Himiko* and are similar in design but have their own unique features. As you ride along, an audio recording will play, talking about some of the various landmarks you're passing. However, the audio is entirely in Japanese, and no English versions or transcriptions are provided (at least that I could find when I went). Still, it's cool to take a picture of the boat and then go back home to your friends and say, "Look what I rode in!"

Just outside Asakusa, you can also find Tokyo Skytree, the tallest tower and second-tallest freestanding structure in the world (more on this in Chapter 19).

WARNING

However, if you plan on visiting Tokyo Skytree, I recommend catching the train. You can see Tokyo Skytree pretty clearly from Senso-ji, so much so that you may be tempted just to walk because it looks so close. However, its height is deceiving. I promise it's not as close as it looks. Can you tell I learned this the hard way?

Bunkyo: The Local Neighborhood

If you're looking to get away from some of the super touristy locations and instead get more of a feel for "living like a local," I recommend checking out the Bunkyo area.

Some of the most popular attractions within Bunkyo are the gardens:

>> **Higo Hosokawa Garden:** Formerly Shin-Edogawa Garden, this garden is a great place to visit if you just need some peace and quiet. Like many other Japanese gardens, a pond serves as the focal point, and other dirt paths lead you around the rest of the garden. Up some stone steps, you can even get a good vantage point of the entire garden.

>> **Koishikawa Korakuen:** This park is a great place for heron viewing, so it's not uncommon to see photographers camped out along the sides of the path. In the pond, you can also find some large koi fish and a turtle or two bathing in the sun. It also has a pond frequently filled with beautiful water lilies.

>> **Rikugien:** This garden is quite large in comparison to some of the other parks and gardens in Tokyo, and is often considered one of Tokyo's most beautiful landscape gardens. It's a great place to take a stroll, and with enough wandering, you'll eventually come upon a high point where you can get a good view of the park below as well as the city in the background.

Right across the street from Higo Hosokawa Garden is Hotel Chinzanso. The hotel itself is nice, but the real reason to visit is for its public garden around back. It offers not only a beautiful waterfall but also a sacred tree, said to be some 500 years old!

Aside from parks and gardens, there are a few other popular attractions in Bunkyo, including Origami Kaikan and Tokyo University.

Origami, the art of paper folding, is a popular part of Japanese culture. At Origami Kaikan, you can see several displays of various origami creations such as dinosaurs, animals, and even dragons. Some are so complex that it's hard to believe they're made from just paper. On the third floor is a shop where you can buy different types of origami paper, as well as instructional books (most of which are in Japanese). You can even take lessons, some of which are offered in multiple languages.

Tokyo University is one of Japan's most prestigious universities (think Harvard or Yale). Students of the university offer campus tours in both Japanese and English and explain not only about some of the historically significant points on campus but also anecdotes about daily student life.

Akihabara: The Tech and Electronics District

Akihabara, often shortened to just Akiba, is primarily famous for its electronic shops. However, it has also become the center for *anime* (animated TV shows and movies) and *manga* (comic books and graphic novels).

If you need anything electronic, Akihabara is the place to go. Here you find large electronic stores such as Yodobashi Camera, Sofmap, Laox, Yamada Denki, and more. If you need to pick up a Japanese SIM card for your phone (see Chapter 3) or outlet and voltage converters (see Chapter 13), you'll want to check here first.

WARNING

Before you get carried away with all the cool electronics and go on a major shopping spree, I highly recommended reading the instructions (or speaking to an English-speaking staff member). Due to electrical and voltage requirements, many electronics may not work outside of Japan.

Video game lovers will want to check out Super Potato, which specializes in vintage video games, consoles, and other collectibles. However, be aware that the same rule applies here as applies to electronics: Many video games purchased in Japan will not work on gaming consoles bought outside Japan.

Anime and manga lovers will be super excited by all the various anime-related shops in Akihabara. Here you can find all sorts of trinkets, posters, stickers, figurines, card games, and other merchandise from popular anime and manga. The only downside is that if your favorite anime or manga isn't particularly popular at the moment, you may have trouble finding related merchandise. Some of the larger anime and manga stores in Akihabara include Mandarake, Akihabara Gamers, Animate, and Akihabara Radio Kaikan.

Akihabara also is famous for its themed cafes. The most popular are the maid cafes, where staff often dress up in maid costumes and treat you like the master of the house instead of a cafe patron. Other popular themed cafes in Akihabara include the Gundam Cafe, designed to immerse guests in the world of Gundam (a popular media franchise featuring giant robots called *gundam*), and AKB48 Cafe and Shop, featuring items from one of Japan's most popular all-female idol groups.

Even if you're not into the "geek" culture Akihabara has become famous for, I recommend stopping here if only to check out 2k540 Aki-Oka Artisan. This arts-and-crafts shopping precinct features shops full of handmade items and superior craftsmanship.

Ueno: The Leisure Area

Ueno is located in the working class area of Tokyo and has more of a laid-back feel to it than some of the other larger shopping and entertainment districts. Don't let that fool you, though. There is still plenty to do here, including Ueno Park and Ameyoko.

Ueno Park is often considered to be one of Japan's first public parks. It has many spacious fields that make for good places to have a picnic or throw a baseball around. It's also famous for the many museums found within the park, including

>> Tokyo National Museum

>> The National Museum for Western Art

>> Tokyo Metropolitan Art Museum

>> The National Science Museum

The other popular attraction in Ueno is Ameya Yokocho, often shortened to just Ameyoko. It's a street lined with all sorts of shops, from general goods to souvenirs to food. It's probably best known for its candy sweets. Because most of the stalls are open, you can even watch them make much of the food. One of the shopkeepers gave me a demonstration on how they made their special honey and peanut cookies. Yum!

Odaiba: Tokyo's Man-Made Island

Odaiba is home to many of the Olympic venues (see Chapter 5), so depending on which sporting events you choose to see, you may end up spending a significant amount of time here. Thankfully, Odaiba has more to offer than just sporting venues.

One of the most notable sights in Odaiba is Rainbow Bridge, which you'll likely cross as you make your way to Odaiba from Tokyo. It's a two-story bridge, and it's quite stunning in the evening when it's all lit up.

Palette Town is one of the more popular shopping and entertainment districts in Odaiba. However, it's probably most notable for its Ferris wheel. At 115 meters (377 feet) tall, it broke the record for the world's tallest Ferris wheel back in 1999. Although it quickly lost that title the following year, it's still one of the largest Ferris wheels in the world.

Also in Odaiba is teamLab Planets and teamLab Borderless. teamLab is an art collective that combines art, science, technology, and design. I'm not normally a big fan of art galleries, but teamLab galleries are absolutely stunning. Words cannot describe how amazing these digital arts galleries are, so I suggest heading over to Google's image search (http://images.google.com) and entering **Tokyo teamLab** to see for yourself.

Chapter **12**

Building an Itinerary

Building an itinerary is one of my favorite things to do during the trip-planning process! However, I know there are plenty of other travelers out there who hate having a set itinerary and just prefer to go where the wind takes them. If that's you, keep in mind that, with the Tokyo 2020 Olympics, many places will be very crowded, so you'll want to make sure you make it to the various events you plan on spectating in time. As such, having at least the *outline* of an itinerary will make your trip go much smoother.

Starting with a Template

Sometimes the hardest part of creating an itinerary is just getting started. I write down things of interest or hotel information on random pieces of scrap paper that I always manage to lose. Itinerary templates are a great solution, because all you have to do is fill in the various pieces of information in the correct spots and — *boom!* — you have a booklet with all the important information.

Every traveler is different, so you may find that you like certain templates better than others. Microsoft Office (`https://templates.office.com/en-us/itineraries`) is a good place to start when looking for travel itinerary templates because it has a large selection with a wide variety of templates. Etsy is another good place, although those templates usually cost money. I even created a template of my own based on my own travel research preferences — you can download it for free at `https://footstepsofadreamer.com/itinerary-template`.

Alternatively, you can pick up the Japan Planning Calendar (`https://pretraveller.com/japan-planning-calendar`), which includes monthly calendars with information specific for Japan to help you plan out your trip.

Filling in the Knowns

After you've found a template, it's time to get started building your itinerary! Often, it's easier to start with the things that are already set in stone. This includes anything booked in advance that isn't easily changed. Because these things aren't flexible in terms of day and time, you'll want to jot them down first and then build the rest of your itinerary around these items. Things such as your flight, hotel reservations, and event tickets will all fall into this category.

Booked flights

After you have your flight booked (see Chapter 10), you'll know exactly how much time you have in Japan. You can't exactly plan to attend a sporting event at 10 a.m. if your plane doesn't land until 2 p.m.

Many itinerary templates have an area for you to fill in all the flight details. Make sure to jot down the airline, flight number, departing time, and arriving time. If you have space, it may also be worth jotting down your gate and seat number if you know it. (The gate and seat assignment aren't necessary, but sometimes it's just nice to have all your information in one place instead of having to pull up your flight confirmation email to find it.)

Over the years, I've also found it beneficial to write down other information specific to the particular airline I'll be flying with. For example, some airlines, especially for international flights, allow the first checked bag for free, some airlines offer free snacks and drinks, and so on. Having this information on hand makes packing (see Chapter 4) and preparing for the flight just a bit easier.

Reserved hotels

Accommodations reservations (see Chapter 10) are typically a bit more flexible than flights, but not always. Especially for the Olympics, many popular hotels aren't offering a free cancellation policy as they normally would. This means that after your reservation is made, you likely won't be able to change it without losing a significant amount of money.

One of the first important pieces of information to jot down is the location of the hotel. The hotel's location will be a big factor in how long it will take you to get to your various destinations and ultimately affect how much time you have to do different activities during the day.

Depending on how much you struggled to find a place to stay, your hotel location may be less than ideal. This means that you may spend a significant amount of time on the train just to get to your destination. Given the popularity of the Tokyo 2020 Olympics, it's to be expected. Just make sure to plan accordingly.

The second most important piece of information is the nearest train station or bus stop to your hotel. Most hotels are within walking distance of a train station. Knowing which train stations are nearby will make figuring out the best route (see Chapter 15) to get to your activities much, much easier.

Your hotel notes may look something like this:

>> **Name:** Tokyu Stay Shinjuku

>> **Address:** 160-0022 Tokyo Prefecture, Shinjuku-ku, Shinjuku 3-7-1, Japan

>> **Check-in:** 3 p.m. on July 24, 2020

>> **Check-out:** 11 a.m. on August 10, 2020

>> **Room type:** 1 full bed

>> **Free cancellation:** Before 11:59 p.m. on July 22, 2020

>> **Nearest station:** Shinjuku Station

>> **Amenities:** Private bathroom, refrigerator, luggage storage, free Wi-Fi, English-speaking staff

Purchased Olympics tickets

You're going to Japan to watch the Olympics, right? So, naturally, the various sporting events you have tickets to will be important activities on your itinerary. You'll definitely want to make sure you get these events blocked off and give yourself plenty of time to get there.

TIP

The Tokyo Organizing Committee of the Olympic and Paralympic Games recommends using public transit in order to get between the venues. They also warn that it may take longer to get to the venues than the times given online and in travel apps due to the high volume of traffic. When putting together your itinerary, make sure to not only block off time for the sporting event, but also to block off plenty of time to get to and leave the venue.

Filling in the Gaps

Now you get to look at your itinerary and see what time you have to explore the rest of Tokyo and Japan. Then you get to start figuring out how you want to fill in these gaps.

It's typically easiest to just start researching things to do in the Tokyo area. I'd start with Chapters 11 and 19 of this book. Japan Guide (www.japan-guide.com), TripAdvisor (www.tripadvisor.com/Home-g294232), and Lonely Planet (www.lonelyplanet.com/japan) are also good places to start brainstorming ideas. For more in-depth recommendations and opinions, you can read personal stories from people who have spent a significant amount of time in Tokyo and Japan as a whole:

>> My own blog posts about Japan are at https://footstepsofadreamer.com/caregory/japan.

>> This book's technical editor, Anne Sutherland-Smith, has written about Japan at https://pretraveller.com/start-here-japan.

>> The blog You Could Travel has information on Japan at www.youcouldtravel.com/destinations/asia/japan.

The key here is to write down anything and everything that looks interesting, regardless of price, location, and any other factor that may sway you to leave it off your list. However, when you write down the activity of interest, make sure to also note all the other relevant information. It will be handy later.

At the end, your notes may look something like this:

>> Hama Rikyu Gardens

- **Location:** Chuo, Tokyo
- **Hours:** Monday–Friday, 9 a.m. to 5 p.m. (entry until 4:30 p.m.)
- **Price:** ¥300 ($2.75)
- **Duration:** 1.5 hours
- **Nearest station(s):** Shiodome Station, JR Shimbashi Station

>> Senso-ji

- **Location:** Taito, Tokyo
- **Hours:** Main hall 6:30 a.m. to 5 p.m., temple grounds always open
- **Price:** Free
- **Duration:** 1 hour
- **Nearest station(s):** Asakusa Station

TIP

I recommend plotting all the points of interest on a map so that you can visually see where all of them are located. I usually do this with Google's My Maps (www.google.com/mymaps). You can see an example of one of these maps for seven days' worth of activities at https://bit.ly/2M8Ph5E.

After you have a visual, it gets easier to see which places are the outliers. Then you can start asking yourself, "Is it really worth going that far just for one activity?" Sometimes the answer is 100 percent yes because it's something you really want to do. Other times, you may think to yourself, "Nah, it's not worth it" and remove the item from your list.

I recommend looking at prices next. How much would it cost for you to do all the activities on your list? Can you afford that?

Granted, not everything on your list may actually fit into your itinerary, so the total cost of attractions on your list may not equate to how much you would actually spend. However, it's a good opportunity to remove some of the truly expensive items from your list.

Also, keep in mind that some places offer discount passes, meaning that some attractions may not have to be as expensive as they may seem at first. Unfortunately, Tokyo doesn't really have a sightseeing pass (as some other major cities in the world do). However, if you plan on taking a day trip or traveling farther outside of Tokyo, items such as the Osaka Amazing Pass, the Nikko Pass, and the Hakone Free Pass may get you discounts on some of your activities.

Sometimes, though, some of the most expensive items on the list are the things you want to do the most. In this case, I would see if you can start removing the items that aren't of as much interest so that only the attractions you truly want to visit and feel would be worth the money are left on your list.

After you get your list of attractions down to a manageable amount, it starts to feel like the game Tetris. The challenge is to figure out which activity will fit in which gap on your itinerary that isn't ridiculously far from the other things you plan to do that day. I usually find it easiest to start with a particular gap in the itinerary, look at what else is on the list for the day, and then compare it to my list of desired activities to see which activity is closest. After I narrow down the list based on location, I figure out which activity will best fit in the gap based on the expected length of time it will take to do the activity, the location's hours of operation, and how long it will take to get to and from the location (see Chapter 15 for how to calculate travel time).

When it's all said and done, you should have a finalized itinerary looking something like Table 12-1 and Table 12-2.

TABLE 12-1 **Day 1 Itinerary**

Time	Activity
Morning	Eat breakfast.
	Take the Oedo line from Shinjuku Station to Shiodome Station.
	Explore Hama Rikyu Gardens.
Afternoon	Take the Oedo line from Shiodome Station to Akabanebashi Station.
	Eat lunch.
	Visit Tokyo Tower.
	Take the JR Yamanote line from Hamamatsuchō Station to Yūrakuchō Station.
Evening	Eat dinner.
	Watch Men's Weightlifting 67 kg.

TABLE 12-2 **Day 2 Itinerary**

Time	Activity
Morning	Eat breakfast.
	Take the Oedo line from Shinjuku Station to Kokuritsu-Kyōgijō Station.
	Watch Track and Field events.
Afternoon	Eat lunch.
	Take the Oedo line from Kokuritsu-Kyōgijō Station to Tochōmae Station.
	Visit Tokyo Metropolitan Government Building observation decks.
Evening	Explore downtown Shinjuku.
	Eat dinner.

4
Enjoying Your Time in Tokyo

Get through the airport.

Learn some useful words and phrases in Japanese.

Find out how to use the different modes of public transit.

Get comfortable with customs and cultural norms.

IN THIS CHAPTER

» Navigating Customs

» Adjusting to the time zone

» Paying with cash and card

» Dealing with electricity differences

» Knowing what to do in an emergency

Chapter 13

Arriving and Getting Oriented

Maybe this is your first time traveling abroad, or maybe it's your hundredth time. Regardless of how frequently you travel, it doesn't change the fact that leaving the country means stepping out of the comfort of home. Many things in Japan will be the same as what you're used to, but some things will be different. Being aware of and preparing for those differences will go a long way toward helping you get adjusted.

Getting through Immigration and Customs

When you arrive at the airport in Japan, you'll need to go through Immigration and Customs, basically telling the Japanese government who you are, why you're there, and what you've brought with you. It's nothing personal — the Japanese government just wants to make sure you're not a security risk.

Filling out the paperwork

While on the plane to Japan, you'll likely be given two forms by a flight attendant: the Disembarkation Card, which is needed when going through Immigration, and the Customs Declaration form, which is for going through Customs. Both cards have Japanese and English instructions and can be filled out in either Japanese or English. If for some reason you aren't given these forms on the plane, you can pick them up in the airport after you land.

Most of the flight attendants are pretty good at explaining who needs to fill out each form. In case they don't, know that one Disembarkation Card is required per person, and one Customs Form is required per family. This means that every person should fill out a Disembarkation Card, but only one person should fill out a Customs Declaration form for the whole family.

The Disembarkation Card

On the Disembarkation Card, you're required to provide the following information:

>> Your *family name* (last name)

>> Your *given name* (first name)

>> Your date of birth

>> Your home city and country

>> The purpose of your visit (tourism, business, visiting relatives, or other)

>> Your last flight number (the flight number for the flight you took to Japan, not the flight number of any previous connecting flights)

>> How long you plan to stay in Japan

>> Where you'll stay in Japan (your hotel address)

>> Any history of receiving a deportation order or refusal of entry into Japan

>> Any history of being convicted of a crime (not just in Japan)

>> Whether you possess controlled substances, guns, bladed weapons, or gunpowder

The Customs Declaration form

The Customs Declaration form will require you to fill out similar personal and travel information as the Disembarkation Card (see the preceding section). It also asks several questions regarding what you're bringing with you to Japan, including the following:

WARNING

>> **Whether you're bringing any prohibited articles and/or restricted articles into Japan:** *Prohibited articles* are items that cannot be brought into Japan at all. *Restricted articles* are items that can be brought into Japan but have restrictions.

The prohibited and restricted articles lists may be changed or updated by the Customs and Tariff Bureau at any time. So, check the Japan Customs website (www.customs.go.jp/english/summary/passenger.htm) before you depart for your trip to ensure that you aren't bringing any prohibited or restricted items with you.

>> **Whether you're bringing gold bullion or products of gold into Japan.**

>> **Whether you're bringing any goods that exceed duty-free allowance in Japan:** In general, personal effects and items for personal use are free of duties and/or taxes. This includes clothes, toiletries, and portable professional equipment. Alcoholic beverages and tobacco products can be brought into Japan duty-free up to a specific amount. Lastly, the total overseas market value of your items must be under ¥200,000 ($1,834.86).

>> **Whether you're bringing commercial goods or samples into Japan:** Basically, anything that you plan to sell or is not for personal use will be subject to duties and/or taxes.

>> **Whether you're bringing any items that someone else has asked you to bring to Japan:** If you're bringing something with you because somebody else asked you to, you'll need to answer yes to this question. However, it's mostly just a check to make sure that you're not unintentionally (or intentionally) smuggling something into the country because somebody asked you to.

>> **Whether you're bringing the equivalent of ¥1,000,000 ($9,174.31) or more into the country (including cash, checks, promissory notes, precious metals, and so on):** There is no limit to the amount of money that can be brought into Japan. However, if you bring the equivalent of ¥1,000,000 ($9,174.31) into Japan, it must be declared.

>> **Whether you have any *unaccompanied articles* (any items you bring into Japan outside of what will be with you at the airport):** For example, if you chose to ship or forward your luggage ahead of you, any luggage you shipped would be considered an unaccompanied article.

Checked luggage is not considered unaccompanied articles. You may not have your checked luggage with you on the plane when you're filling out this paperwork, but you'll pick up your luggage before going through Customs at the airport.

Going through Quarantine and Immigration

When you get off the plane, the first section you'll come to in the airport is Quarantine. Unless a medical questionnaire form was distributed on the plane, you won't have to do anything here. Most times, passengers are only required to go through Quarantine when they're coming from areas dealing with certain outbreaks. For example, passengers coming to Japan from North America were required to go through Quarantine during the H1N1 outbreak back in 2009 and 2010.

After Quarantine is the Immigration section. Here, you need to present your passport and Disembarkation Card.

Also, all those who are granted permission for short-term stay (without a visa) will be photographed, fingerprinted, and asked for proof of onward travel or proof that they'll be leaving the country.

During the off-season, many travelers can get through Immigration in less than 20 minutes. However, during popular travel times, such as cherry blossom season, this process can take over an hour due to long lines. With the large influx of travelers for the Olympics, be prepared for the process to take longer than expected. For this reason, I recommend not booking any transportation tickets or activities too close to your flight arrival time.

Going through Customs

After you go through Immigration, you'll find baggage claim, where you can pick up any luggage you may have checked. Also near here, you'll find the plant and animal quarantine area. You need to stop here if you're bringing animals, meats, fruits, or other plants into Japan.

After you have your bags, continue forward and you'll arrive at Customs. Here, you find two different lines: Green Channel and Red Channel. The Green Channel is for those who do not have anything to declare. The Red Channel is for those who do have items to declare or aren't sure.

Regardless of which line you choose, you'll be asked to present your passport and Customs Declaration form. Most times, Customs officers will conduct a high-level interview, asking questions such as "Where are you from?," "How long are you staying?," or "Are you bring X, Y, or Z item with you?"

On occasion, travelers have been asked additional, more in-depth questions and even had their bags searched. This may become more common as Japan increases security to ensure the safety of visitors during the Olympics.

Adapting to the Time Change

The change in time zone is one of the first and likely most challenging things you'll have to adjust to upon arriving in Japan. Depending on where you live, you may have anywhere from a 1-hour time difference to a 17-hour time difference, which means jet lag may or may not come into play.

Knowing Japan's time zone: Japan Standard Time

Japan operates on Japan Standard Time (JST), which is 9 hours ahead of Coordinated Universal Time (UTC).

WARNING

Unlike some parts of the world, Japan does not observe daylight saving time, meaning that the clocks do not jump forward or backward. It stays the exact same the entire year. This means the time difference between Japan and other parts of the world may vary depending on the time of year.

Take the East Coast of the United States, for example. During Eastern Daylight Time (EDT), Japan is 13 hours ahead, but during Eastern Standard Time (EST), Japan is 14 hours ahead. The same goes for the United Kingdom. Japan is 8 hours ahead of British Summer Time (BST), but 9 hours ahead of Greenwich Mean Time (GMT).

For 2020 in the United States, daylight saving time begins on March 8 and ends on November 1. If you only plan on visiting Japan for the Olympics, you won't have to worry about the changing difference in time zones. However, if you plan on extending your trip in Japan for a while, you'll need to keep it in mind.

Overcoming jetlag

You'll probably have to cope with jet lag, but there are ways to help reduce the effects.

The first is simply to be prepared and know what to expect. For example, did you know that jet lag tends to be worse when you're traveling east (in terms of time zones)?

So, if you're departing from the West Coast of the United States, you may physically travel west to arrive in Japan, but in terms of time zones, you're technically traveling east. I know it's confusing, but long story short, be aware that your jet lag will likely be worse on your way *to* Japan than it will be on your way back.

The general rule of thumb is that jet lag recovery takes one day for every time zone crossed. That means that if you're traveling to Japan from the United States or Canada, it could take two to two and a half weeks to fully recover from jet lag! However, you most likely will only be in Japan for a few weeks, so needing up to two and a half weeks to recover from jet lag isn't really feasible. You'd recover from jet lag just in time to get back on a plane and jump several time zones again. Thankfully, there are plenty of things you can do to help minimize the impact of jet lag.

Start adjusting in advance

One of the best things you can do to combat jet lag is to start adjusting to your new time zone in advance. Having a flight that departs first thing in the morning will help with this.

For example, let's say that you have a flight that departs from New York City on July 24 at 6 a.m. EDT. Instead of going to bed around your normal time the night before your flight (say, 10 p.m. EDT), your best bet is to stay up all night. Yes, *all night*.

This is because 10 p.m. EDT on July 23 (the night before your flight) is 11 a.m. on July 24 in Japan. By not letting yourself fall asleep until 6:30 a.m. EDT on July 24, after you've boarded your flight and taken off, you'll be "going to bed" at 7:30 p.m. JST. While 7:30 p.m. isn't exactly an ideal time to go to sleep for the night, it at least gets you closer to being on Japan time. Plus, by staying up all night, you'll likely have an easier time falling asleep on the plane, which will make the long flight go by quicker.

Keep moving

The second-best thing you can do is hit the ground running after you land. Under no circumstances should you let yourself take a nap during the day (unless of course you're going to pass out on the street — don't do that).

For those struggling with jet lag, taking a nap will only lengthen the effects of the jet lag.

It's not uncommon for travelers to say that they're going to take a "half-hour nap" and then accidentally sleep for five hours. Yes, I was 100 percent referring to myself in that last sentence. My third day in Japan, I decided to take a nap at 2 p.m. JST and woke up at 7 p.m. JST. Suffice it to say, I didn't sleep much that night.

By taking a nap (especially a long nap), you basically throw any progress you made toward overcoming jet lag out the window.

The easiest way to avoid the urge to take a nap is simply to not let yourself be bored (hence, my advice to hit the ground running). You'll find that it's much easier to accidentally take a nap if you're sitting around your hotel room instead of being out and about exploring the town.

If you can't be out adventuring for whatever reason, at least try not to sit inside. Sunlight helps your body adjust to your new time zone. There's some fancy science as to why this is so, but all that's really important is that you try to be outside as much as possible because sunlight tells your body it's not time to go to sleep yet.

Avoid dehydrating substances

Every now and then, you may hear people talking about ordering a glass of wine on the plane to help them get to sleep. Unfortunately, dehydration can make jet lag symptoms worse. Alcohol may help you initially get to sleep, but the dehydration it can cause may come back around to bite you in the end. Avoid caffeine for the same reason. Instead, focus on drinking plenty of water.

Managing Your Money

You may be surprised to learn that cash is still king in Japan. At home, you may be used to carrying very little cash with you, if any at all. However, in Japan, you'll likely use cash pretty much everywhere. As such, it's definitely worth familiarizing yourself with the Japanese yen (JPY), the official currency of Japan.

Knowing how much what you've got is worth

The exchange rate between the U.S. dollar (USD) and JPY changes daily (as it does between all currencies).

Back in June 2015, travelers could get ¥125 for $1. In August 2016, it dropped as low as ¥100 for $1. More recently, in November 2019, it hovered around ¥109 for $1.

When standing in a souvenir shop trying to figure out how much an item will cost in your home currency, it can get annoying having to look up the exchange rate and then do some division to figure out how much a souvenir costs.

TIP

If you have a smartphone, download a currency conversion app. Just go to your phone's app store, and search for "currency converter." You'll find several good options that'll make traveling in Japan (or anywhere) easier.

TIP

If you're converting JPY to USD, you can do some quick math for converting. Many travelers find it easy to just assume that ¥100 is about $1. Then you can look at a price tag in yen and drop the last two zeros (or move the decimal point two places to the left) and roughly get the USD equivalent. You may get a little more than ¥100 per dollar, but this gives you a ballpark estimate on the fly.

Making sense of the Japanese yen

If you're anything like me, you may drop change in donation jars at registers, throw coins in a cup holder in your car, or lose them in the couch. Some people hold onto coins and put them in a piggy bank, but there are definitely a significant number of people who find change more annoying than useful.

If you're one of the many people who hate using change, you may have to rethink the way you look at coins when you're in Japan. Americans are used to the $1 bill and $5 bill, while Europeans are used to the €5 bill, and Australians are used to the $5 bill. The equivalent in Japanese yen are coins. That's right, the ¥100 and ¥500 are *coins*. This means that if you start casually throwing coins to the side as you're used to doing, you may be throwing away a significant chunk of change!

I recommend at least somewhat familiarizing yourself with the various coins. I had a hard time distinguishing between the ¥5 and ¥50 coins, especially when digging through a coin purse looking for a specific one. The two coins are supposed to be different colors, but depending on how old and worn the coins are, they can sometimes start to look the same. Thankfully, all but the ¥5 yen coin has its value written in roman characters on at least one of the sides. If you look at a coin and don't see a number on either side, that's the ¥5 coin!

The banknotes or "bills" are similar to what you'll find in other countries. The ¥1,000 bill is roughly equivalent to the $10 bill in the United States, the ¥5,000 bill is the same as a $50 bill, and the ¥10,000 yen bill is equivalent to a $100 bill.

Interestingly enough, Japan does technically have a ¥2,000 bill, but it's rare. In terms of value, it's about the same as a $20 bill, but in terms of rarity, it's more like a $2 bill. In the United States, many people have never seen a $2 bill, or they've only seen it once or twice. The same goes for the ¥2,000 bill in Japan. Some people have seen it, but only rarely.

If you choose to exchange money before your trip (more on this in the next section), you may end up receiving several ¥2,000 bills from your bank. Despite their rarity, they're legal currency and they can be used almost everywhere. On occasion, you may find a vending machine or ticketing machine that has not been programmed to accept them, but even this is becoming less common.

Getting cash

In general, banks will likely provide some of the best exchange rates, and currency exchange shops found in airports and other popular tourist destinations will likely provide the worst.

You'll need to decide whether you want to exchange money before you leave home, after you arrive in Japan, or both.

Before your trip

REMEMBER

I recommend stopping by your local bank before your trip to exchange at least some money. Having Japanese yen in hand (okay, maybe not in your hand, but in one of your bags or something) will likely take some stress off when you first land. You won't have to run around the airport trying to find a place where you can exchange money without getting a terrible exchange rate.

TIP

You don't need to exchange enough money for your entire trip, but I recommend getting enough cash to at least get you through the first day or two. This will allow you to get to your hotel and get settled before worrying about trying to find a place to get cash.

WARNING

Your home bank will probably have to order Japanese yen — very few banks have it on hand. It will typically take about 24 to 48 hours to arrive, so if you want to exchange cash before your trip, you'll definitely want to do this at least a couple of days before you depart.

While you're at the bank, speak with them about possible fees that you can incur while traveling and see if they have any options that would allow you to avoid fees (more on this in the next section).

While in Japan

After you arrive in Japan, the best place to withdraw cash will be from ATMs, because that's where you get the best exchange rate. However, not every ATM will accept cards that have been issued overseas. The best places for travelers to withdraw money will be at the ATMs found in post offices and 7-Eleven stores. In larger areas such as Tokyo, Kyoto, and similar cities, a post office or 7-Eleven always seems to be within a few minutes' walk. Even in more rural areas, a post office or 7-Eleven likely won't be super difficult to find.

The availability of ATMs within post offices varies depending on the office, but at the very minimum they'll be available during the day, typically 9 a.m. to 4 p.m. However, ATMs at larger post offices may be available as long as 7 a.m. to 11 p.m. Also note that the ATMs in post offices are unavailable on Sundays and holidays.

7-Eleven ATMs are typically available 24 hours a day, 7 days a week, 365 days a year (with some exceptions). Visa cards are accepted 24 hours a day, but MasterCard is accepted only from 12:10 a.m. to 11:50 p.m. Other accepted credit cards, such as American Express and Discover, have similar limitations.

ATMs that accept international cards can also be found at other select convenience stores such as Family Mart and Lawsons and can also be found in airports and major department stores.

If you have the option, I recommend going to 7-Eleven ATMs when possible because they don't charge an ATM fee. Post office ATMs and other ATMs that accept international cards may charge up to ¥216 ($1.98) per withdrawal.

WARNING

On top of the ATM fee, many banks charge an additional fee for withdrawing money abroad. Sometimes it's a flat rate, sometimes it's a percentage of the amount withdrawn, and sometimes it's both. For example, a bank may charge a $5 international ATM fee plus a foreign transaction fee equal to 3 percent of the transaction amount; those fees will show up on your bank statement every time you withdraw money in Japan.

TIP

Before your trip, I recommend talking to your home bank regarding what fees you may incur while in Japan. Many banks offer premium accounts or travel cards that don't incur international fees (but have other stipulations). It's worth talking to your bank to determine the best option for you.

Using Credit and Debit Cards

One of the first questions that comes to mind for those who travel internationally is, "Can I use my credit or debit card?"

Before I tackle that question, though, I want to discuss which card you should use.

TIP

As a general rule of thumb, I recommend using a credit card instead of a debit card when making purchases and only using a debit card when withdrawing cash from an ATM.

Debit cards simply don't offer the same protections as credit cards when it comes to things such as identity theft and compromised cards. Plus, it's significantly harder to get money back when fraudulent charges are made against a debit card instead of a credit card. I discuss withdrawing cash in the previous section, so going forward I'm going to specifically focus on credit cards.

So, let's go back to the original question. Can you pay for things in Japan with a credit card? The short answer is: Sometimes.

As mentioned in the previous section, Japan is a very cash-driven society. However, there are a few places where credit cards are accepted. The most common one is accommodations. Most hotels and hostels will accept credit cards. Large train stations are another location where you may be able to use your card. The ticket machines are often cash only, but the larger train stations will have ticket offices where you can use a credit card. Lastly, you may find various large department stores, restaurants, and souvenirs shops that accept credit cards, but usually only in major cities and tourist areas.

The two largest credit cards in Japan are Visa and MasterCard and are accepted at most locations that accept credit cards. Japan's local credit card brand, JCB, is also widely accepted. For other credit card brands, such as American Express and Discover, acceptance is hit or miss. Many stores that accept credit cards have stickers of the brands that are accepted in a front window or by the cash register. However, I always recommend asking the staff to confirm that a particular credit card is accepted before you begin eating or shopping (because some places may only accept credit cards during certain times of the day).

TIP

The other thing to keep in mind is that some credit cards charge foreign transaction fees. Thankfully, most travel credit cards wave the fee. I recommend checking with your bank to see whether you'll be charged any additional fees when using your card abroad.

REMEMBER

If you choose to pay for something with a credit card, you may be asked whether you would like to pay with Japanese yen or your home currency. Always, *always* choose to pay with Japanese yen. The only benefit of paying in your home currency is that you get to see the specific amount that you're going to be charged in a currency you're familiar with. The downsides to paying with your home currency greatly outweigh this small benefit.

When you choose to pay with local currency (Japanese yen), your bank will set the exchange rate. However, if you choose to pay with your home currency, dynamic currency conversion comes into play. You get an exchange rate that is set by a third party and is typically lower than what is offered by banks. On top of that, you get charged an extra fee (typically a percentage of the total transaction) for the convenience of being able to see the amount charged in your home currency. Long story short, you'll end up paying more in the end if you choose to pay in your home currency instead of the local one. It can really add up if you're making large purchases such as paying for lodging.

Honestly, I recommend just using cash whenever possible and only keeping a credit card and debit card with you in case of an emergency. Thankfully, Japan is relatively safe. I never carry more than $40 to $60 on me at any given time when I'm in the United States, but in Japan I felt perfectly comfortable carrying $200 or more around with me. Just be smart about it, and don't wave it around.

Also, don't forget to notify your bank and credit card company in advance that you'll be traveling so your account doesn't get locked while you're abroad!

WARNING

Using IC Cards

IC Cards are cards that can be loaded with cash and then used for payment at some locations. Most people use them to pay for the train and bus instead of paying for individual tickets, but some shops and vending machines also accept IC Cards as forms of payment. If you don't want to pay with a credit card but you also don't want to keep large amounts of cash on hand, an IC Card is a great alternative. Just take care not to lose it!

IC Cards can be obtained from ticket kiosks found within train stations around Japan. They typically cost ¥2,000 ($18.35). ¥500 ($4.59) is used as a deposit for the card itself. The other ¥1,500 ($13.76) is loaded onto the card for you to begin using. If you return the IC Card at the end of your trip, you'll receive your ¥500 ($4.60) deposit back. However, because IC Cards are valid for ten years, it may be worth holding onto if you plan to return to Japan in the future.

TIP

Some train stations have begun offering IC Cards specifically for tourists. These IC Cards don't have the ¥500 ($4.59) deposit, but they're only valid for 28 days.

There are various brands of IC Cards, such as Iococa, Pasmo, Suica, and more. However, the only difference between the brands is who they're sold by and who they can be returned to. For example, if you purchase an IC Card from a ticket kiosk at a Japan Rail (JR) line in Tokyo, you'll likely receive a Suica card, the JR East Company's brand of IC Card. This means that if you intend to return the IC Card at the end of your trip to receive your deposit back, you can only return the card to a JR East station. Other than this fact, the various IC Card brands can be used interchangeably.

Plugging In: Electricity in Japan

If you've never traveled outside your home country before, you may be surprised to discover that electrical outlets and voltage are not the same everywhere you go. Better to discover it now, rather than arrive in Japan and realize a bit late that you can't charge your electronics (although it's not impossible to buy adapters and converters in Japan).

Electrical outlets and adapters

Fifteen different types of electrical outlets are used around the world. The U.S. Department of Commerce International Trade Administration (ITA) has conveniently labeled the different outlets from A to O. In the United States and Canada, you'll typically see Type A plugs (two flat prongs) and Type B plugs (two flat prongs and one round prong).

Conveniently, Japan also uses Type A and Type B plugs. However, Type A plugs are definitely more common than Type B in Japan. In general, you probably won't need an adapter when traveling to Japan if you're from the United States. However, if you have a lot of electronic devices that are Type B plugs, it may be worth picking up an adapter.

Voltage and converters

In the United States and Canada, the standard voltage is 120 volts. In Japan, the standard is 100 volts. The difference in voltage can be handled by most electronics. You may just find that your electronic devices will charge a bit slower than you're used to. However, devices that tend to pull hard on the electricity, such as hairdryers and hair straighteners, may have much more notice-able impact on performance. Luckily, many hotels in Japan pro-vide a hair dryer. If you want to be safe and bring your own, some beauty stores and online shops sell travel versions of hairdryers and straighteners that are dual voltage.

When in doubt, check the tags on your electrical devices. Most will list the required voltage in order to be able to function properly.

Where to buy adapters and converters

If you know in advance that you're going to need an adapter and/or converter for your electrical devices, I recommend ordering them online and having them shipped to you before you leave. You'll typically find the best prices though trusted online retailers such as Amazon and Walmart.

If you don't realize you need an adapter and/or converter until after you arrive in Japan, you'll find that most electronics stores sell adapters and converters. Bic Camera and Yodobashi Camera are two good places to start. Don't let the *Camera* in their names fool you — both sell pretty much all types of electronics.

Staying Safe and Healthy

The last thing anybody wants to think about is something terrible happening while traveling. Thankfully, Japan is considered a very safe country, with a great healthcare system and significantly low crime rates. However, it's still best to be prepared to ensure you stay safe and healthy during your trip to Japan.

Handling emergencies

If you're from the United States, you probably know you should dial 911 for emergencies. This phone number can be used for pretty much any emergency in the United States — criminal, fire, medical, and so on.

In Japan, there are two numbers you'll want to keep in mind. The first one, 119, is for fire and medical emergencies. It should be somewhat easy to remember because it's the inverse of 911. The second phone number to remember is 110, which is the emergency number for the police and to report crimes and accidents.

Finding local doctors and hospitals

Unfortunately, you can't always control where and when you may get sick. (If you can, please share your secret!) In the unfortunate event that you do get sick while in Japan, you'll want to know how to locate the nearest doctor's office or hospital.

TIP

The Japan National Tourism Organization (JNTO) website (www.jnto.go.jp/emergency/eng/mi_guide.html) allows you to search for medical institutions based on medical department (pediatrics, dermatology, and so on), languages spoken, and payment methods accepted. You can also download the list of medical institutions as a PDF; that way, you have a copy of the list available even if you don't have Internet access.

REMEMBER

I recommend purchasing travel medical insurance before your trip. In the unlikely event that you need to visit a doctor or hospital, travel medical insurance will likely save you some hefty medical bills.

If you live in the United States, you may have heard of the concept of PPO networks, where healthcare providers partner with specific insurance programs. However, this concept does not exist outside the United States, so you won't have to worry about finding a healthcare provider who is "in network."

Some travel insurance companies also provide other helpful medical-related travel information, such as healthcare provider locations, medication equivalents, and medical term translations. For example, you likely won't find Advil, a brand of ibuprofen, in Japan. However, your travel insurance provider may be able to help you find an equivalent Japanese brand of ibuprofen.

Chapter **14**

Learning Some Simple Japanese Phrases

Worried about not speaking the native language? No need to fear!

Before the Tokyo 2020 Olympics, there were mixed reports about how easy it was to navigate Tokyo (and Japan as a whole) without any knowledge of Japanese. Some said it was super easy, while others struggled to find English speakers.

Thankfully, with the approaching Olympic Games, many in Japan have made an effort to incorporate English more. Many of the locals are trying to learn at least some useful English phrases, and bilingual volunteers have been in high demand. Japan's tourism authorities have also made a big push to make Tokyo easily accessible for overseas visitors, encouraging the travel industry to create English versions of signs, directions, informational pamphlets, and more.

TIP

However, I strongly believe that those visiting a foreign country should at least *attempt* to learn a bit of the native language. Most locals appreciate the effort, and it can come in handy in the rare event that you find yourself in a situation where there are no English speakers or signs in the vicinity.

This chapter goes over Japanese at an extremely high level and is designed to teach you enough to get out of a tight spot. As such, I also recommend picking up *Japanese For Dummies*, 3rd Edition, by Hiroko M Chiba and Eriko Sato (Wiley). It will help you get a much stronger grasp of the language.

Getting Started with Japanese

Many people see the Japanese writing system and immediately assume it's a super-hard language to learn. I'm here to tell you it's not. Actually, I personally found learning Japanese even easier than learning Spanish or Italian.

The Japanese alphabet

The Japanese alphabet doesn't consist of consonants and vowels like English. Instead, the Japanese alphabet consists of syllables. For example, the character か is read "ka," the character き is read "ki," and the character く is read "ku." Every character (with the exception of one) is a combination of a consonant and a vowel.

You likely won't have to do much writing during your time in Japan, so you won't need to memorize the alphabet, but it's important to have a basic understanding of it because it will help you understand how to properly pronounce Japanese words.

Pronunciation

Thanks to the alphabet being syllable based, most Japanese words are pronounced exactly how they're spelled. No funky words like *colonel* being pronounced "kur-nuhl."

REMEMBER

Japanese syllables are always pronounced the same. In general, their sound doesn't change based on what other consonants or vowels are nearby.

Here are the correct pronunciations of the vowels:

Vowel	Correct Pronunciation
A	"ah" like f**a**ther
E	"eh" like b**e**d

Vowel	Correct Pronunciation
I	"ee" like glorious
O	"oh" like no
U	"oo" like "influence"

With this in mind, the characters か, き, and く mentioned in the previous section are written as "ka," "ki," and "ku," and would be pronounced "kah," "kee," and "koo," respectively.

There are a few exceptions to the rule of syllable pronunciation not changing:

>> Double consonants indicate emphasis.

>> Double vowels extend the sound.

When an *o* is followed by a *u*, the sound should be held a bit longer. For example, the word *byouin* (meaning "hospital") should be pronounced "byo-oh-een."

When you see two consonants, you should add a slight pause. For example, the word *roppyaku* (meaning "six hundred") should be pronounced "rope-pya-koo," almost as if it's two different words. Almost.

WARNING

Lastly, it's important to note that the consonant *r* is pronounced slightly different in Japanese than it is in English. In Japanese, it's pronounced quite softly, almost like a mix between an *l* and an *r* sound.

Pronouncing *r* correctly is something most native English speakers struggle with. Think about the way you softly pronounce the *t* in words like *cutter*. The tip of your tongue just barely touches the top of your mouth. The Japanese *r* is very much like that.

Basic sentence structure

In English, sentences are structured subject-verb-object. Take the sentence *I speak Japanese,* for example:

>> **Subject:** I
>> **Verb:** Speak
>> **Object:** Japanese

However, in Japanese, sentences are structured subject-object-verb. Using the same example, you would say, "I Japanese speak."

Japanese also uses something called *particle markers*. These are "words" that mark various parts of the sentence. For example, は (written as *wa* and pronounced "wah") is used for marking the subject of the sentence and を (written as *o* and pronounced "oh") is used for marking the object. Again returning to the previous example, the sentence would be "I は Japanese を speak."

The Japanese word for *I* is 私 *(watashi)*. The word for *Japanese* is 日本語 *(nihongo)*. The word for *speak* is 話します *(hanashimasu)*. Altogether, the example sentence would be 私は日本語を話します or *Watashi wa nihongo o hanashimasu.*

Saying, "huh?"

WARNING

In English, it's common to say, "Huh?" when you didn't hear what somebody said and want him to repeat it. The first time I did this to one of my Japanese friends, it actually startled him. In Japan, "Haa?" is typically said in an angry tone and has a "Did you really just say that to me right now?" feel to it. When I said "huh?" to my friend in English, he missed the slight difference in pronunciation and thought I was angry at him or that he had offended me in some way. If you need somebody to repeat something, I recommend using the sound "Eh?" to avoid this miscommunication. You could also say "Nani?" meaning "What?"

Knowing the Phrases You Need to Survive

In the next few sections, you find various words and phrases that may come in handy in the various situations you may find yourself when visiting Japan for the Olympics. It's best to try and commit them to memory, but don't forget you can always use this book as a reference, too!

Greetings

Table 14-1 lists words that others may use to greet you, or in the case of the last word on the list, shout at you.

TABLE 14-1 Greetings

English	Japanese Script	Romanized Japanese
Good morning	おはようございます	Ohayou gozaimasu
Good afternoon	こんにちは	Konnichiwa
Good evening	こんばんは	Konbanwa
Welcome	いらっしゃいませ	Irasshaimase

In general, *ohayou gozaimasu* is used in the mornings, *konnichiwa* is used during the day, and *konbanwa* is used in the evenings. However, you'll occasionally hear them used interchangeably. Don't let it throw you off too much.

REMEMBER

If you can't remember any of the other words on this list, remember *Konnichiwa.* Many people use it as a generic "hello," regardless of the time of day.

You'll likely never use *irasshaimase,* because it's a very formal way of saying "welcome." However, waitresses and store attendants will probably say it to you when you walk into a restaurant or store.

Being polite

At home, you probably wouldn't walk up to a stranger and say, "What up, yo?" Or maybe you would, but *most* people wouldn't. It's just considered impolite. Similarly, you'll want to try to be polite to the various people you meet when in Japan. Table 14-2 provides some common phrases.

TABLE 14-2 Being Polite

English	Japanese Script	Romanized Japanese
Thank you	ありがとうございます	Arigatou gozaimasu
Excuse me	すみません	Sumimasen
I'm sorry	ごめんなさい	Gomen nasai
Please remove your shoes	靴は脱いで下さい	Kutsu wa nuide kudasai

The *gozaimasu* in *arigatou gozaimasu* and the *nasai* in *gomen nasai* can technically be omitted, making it a bit less formal. It would be like saying "Thanks" instead of "Thank you." However, it's better to be too polite than not polite enough, so use the whole phrase if you can remember it.

Answers

If somebody asks you a question, you'll want to be able to answer. For now, I'll stick to the simple yes or no answer (see Table 14-3).

TABLE 14-3 **Yes and No**

English	Japanese Script	Romanized Japanese
Yes	はい	Hai
No	いいえ	Iie

Introductions

You likely won't need to introduce yourself when visiting a store or restaurant, but if you make a new friend, you'll want to at least be able to tell her who you are (see Table 14-4).

TABLE 14-4 **Introductions**

English	Japanese Script	Romanized Japanese
My name is [*name*]	私の名前は[*name*]です	Watashi no namae wa [*name*] desu
What is your name?	お名前は何ですか	Onamae wa nan desu ka?
It's nice to meet you	初めまして	Hajimemashite
Where are you from? Where is your hometown?	ご出身はどちらですか	Goshusshin wa dochira desu ka?
I am from [*place*]	私は[*place*]からです	Watashi wa [*place*] kara desu

Directions

Asking for directions will likely be one of the more common things you do in Japan. Table 14-5 has you covered.

TABLE 14-5 Directions

English	Japanese Script	Romanized Japanese
I want to go to [place]	[Place]に行きたいです	[Place] ni ikitai desu
Where is [place]?	[Place]はどこですか	[Place] wa doko desu ka?
Go straight Go forward	真っ直ぐ	Massugu
Right	右	Migi
Left	左	Hidari

"I want to go to [*name of place you want to go*]" will use the format "[*Place name*] ni ikitai desu." All you have to do is drop in the name of the place in the brackets. For example, if you want to go to Fukushima Azuma Baseball Stadium, one of the venues for the Olympics, you would say, "Fukushima Azuma Baseball Stadium ni ikitai desu."

Similarly, you can say, "[*Place name*] wa doko desu ka?" to ask where something is. Using the same example as earlier, you could say, "Fukushima Azuma Baseball Stadium wa doko desu ka?" to ask, "Where is Fukushima Azuma Baseball Stadium?"

Transportation

Navigating Japan's public transportation system is one of the more difficult aspects of traveling to Japan. Knowing a few of the key words can make it easier (see Table 14-6).

TABLE 14-6 Transportation

English	Japanese Script	Romanized Japanese
Train	電車	Denshya
Subway	地下鉄	Chikatetsu
Train station	駅	Eki
Bus	バス	Basu
Bus stop	バス停	Basutei

(continued)

TABLE 14-6 *(continued)*

English	Japanese Script	Romanized Japanese
Local (train)	普通	Futsuu
Rapid or semi-express (train)	快速	Kaisoku
Express (train)	急行	Kyuukou
Limited express (train)	特急	Tokkyuu
Does this train/bus go to [*place*]?	この「電車・バス」は [*place*]に行きますか	Kono denshya/basu wa [*place*] ni ikimasu ka?

TIP

There are usually signs in English that indicate which trains and buses stop at which stations. However, if you want to make sure you're getting on the correct train or bus, you can use the template "Kono denshya/basu wa [*place*] ni ikimasu ka?" to ask if a particular train/bus goes to your destination.

Sports

Given that you'll be in Japan for the Olympics, you'll want to know how to say the different sports in Japanese. Thankfully, most of the words are borrowed from English, so they'll be very similar to what you're used to (see Table 14-7).

TABLE 14-7 Sports

English	Japanese Script	Romanized Japanese
Archery	アーチェリー	A-cherii
Artistic	体操競技	Taisou kyougi
Artistic swimming	アーティスティック スイミング	A-tisutikku suimingu
Aquatics	水泳	Suiei
Athletics	陸上競技	Rikujou kyougi
Badminton	バドミントン	Badominton
Baseball	野球	Yakyuu
Basketball	バスケットボール	Basukettobouru

English	Japanese Script	Romanized Japanese
Beach volleyball	ビーチバレーボール	Biichi Bareibouru
BMX freestyle	BMX フリースタイル	Bi emu ekusu furiisutairu
BMX racing	BMX レーシング	Bi emu ekusu reishingu
Boxing	ボクシング	Bokushingu
Canoe	カヌー	Kanuu
Cycling	自転車競技	Jitensha kyougi
Diving	飛込	Tobikomi
Dressage	馬場馬術	Baba bajutsu
Equestrian	馬術	Bajutsu
Eventing	総合馬術	sougou bajutsu
Fencing	フェンシング	Fenshingu
Golf	ゴルフ	Gorufu
Gymnastics	体操	Taisou
Handball	ハンドボール	Handobouru
Hockey	ホッケー	hokkei
Judo	柔道	Juudou
Jumping	障害馬術	shougai bajutsu
Karate	空手	Karate
Marathon	マラソン	Marason
Marathon swimming	マラソンスイミング	Marason suimingu
Modern pentathlon	近代五種	Kindaigoshu
Mountain bike	マウンテンバイク	Mauntenbaiku
Park	パーク	Paaku
Race walk	競歩	Kyouho
Rhythmic	新体操	Shintaisou
Rifle and pistol	ライフル射撃	Raifuru shageki

(continued)

TABLE 14-7 *(continued)*

English	Japanese Script	Romanized Japanese
Road	ロード	roudo
Rowing	ボート	Bouto
Rugby	ラグビー	Ragubii
Sailing	セーリング	Seiringu
Shooting	射撃	Shageki
Shotgun (clay target)	クレー射撃	Kurei shageki
Skateboarding	スケートボード	sukeitoboudo
Slalom	スラローム	Suraroumu
Soccer	サッカー	Sakkaa
Softball	ソフトボール	Sofutobouru
Sport climbing	スポーツクライミング	Supoutsu kuraimingu
Sprint	スプリント	Supurinto
Street	ストリート	Sutoriito
Surfing	サーフィン	Saafin
Swimming	競泳	Kyouei
Table tennis	卓球	Takkyuu
Tae kwon do	テコンドー	Tekondou
Tennis	テニス	Tenisu
Track	トラック	torakku
Track and field	トラック・フィールド	Torakku fiirudo
Trampoline	トランポリン	Toranporin
Triathlon	トライアスロン	Toraiasuron
Volleyball	バレーボール	Bareibouru
Water polo	水球	Suikyuu
Weightlifting	ウエイトリフティング	Ueitorifutingu
Wrestling	レスリング	Resuringu

Numbers

Chances are, any numbers you come across will be written in roman characters. When you visit shops and restaurants, prices of most items will be written with English numerals (1, 2, 3, and so on). Even when you pay at the register and the attendant tells you how much you owe, the total will likely be displayed on the register in English numerals.

WARNING

On occasion though, when visiting some mom-and-pop restaurants or more traditional stores, you'll see numbers written in the Japanese writing system. Knowing the Japanese numbers can also be helpful when asking how much an item costs or communicating your hotel address. Thankfully, numbers in Japanese are relatively straightforward (see Table 14-8).

TABLE 14-8 Numbers

English	Japanese Script	Romanized Japanese
One	一	Ichi
Two	二	Ni
Three	三	San
Four	四	Yon
Five	語	Go
Six	六	Roku
Seven	七	Nana
Eight	八	Hachi
Nine	九	Kyuu
Ten	十	Juu
Eleven	十一	Juu ichi
Twelve	十二	Juu ni
Thirteen	十三	Juu san

The word *seventeen* would be the combination of the words *ten* and *seven* or "juu nana."

But then how do you count past nineteen? Based on this pattern, can you take a guess as to what *twenty* would be? I'll give you a hint, it's another combination of two words. . . .

If you guessed, "ni juu" or two tens, then you're correct. *Twenty-five* would be "ni juu go," and *thirty-six* would be "san juu roku." See the pattern?

One hundred, or "hyaku," is the first new word you'll encounter that will break the pattern. However, after one hundred, the pattern continues. *One hundred and twenty-one* would be "hyaku ni juu ichi" and *two hundred and two* would be "ni hyaku ni."

WARNING

Note that starting in the hundreds and continuing on into the higher numbers, you'll start encountering words that slightly vary from the pattern (see Table 14-9). You may expect *eight hundred* to be "hachi hyaku," but it's actually "happyaku." The pronunciations of some of the words vary from the pattern to make them easier to pronounce.

TABLE 14-9 ## Higher Numbers

English	Japanese Script	Romanized Japanese
One hundred	百	Hyaku
Two hundred	二百	Ni hyaku
Three hundred	三百	San byaku
Six hundred	六百	Roppyaku
Eight hundred	八百	Happyaku
One thousand	千	Sen
Two thousand	二千	Ni sen
Three thousand	三千	San zen
Eight thousand	八千	Hassen
Ten thousand	万	Man
Twenty thousand	二万	Ni man

Another important fact to point out is that in English, we get a new word every three digits.

(1) One **thousand**

(2) Ten **thousand**

(3) One hundred **thousand**

(1) One **million**

(2) Ten **million**

(3) One hundred **million**

(1) One **billion**

See the pattern? You can also see this based on where we place the comma. For example, one billion is written as 1,000,000,000. The comma is placed after every three digits.

However Japanese is every *four* digits.

(1) One thousand: "**Sen**"

(2) Ten thousand: "**Man**"

(3) One hundred thousand: "Juu **man**" (ten ten-thousands)

(1) One million: "Hyaku **man**" (one hundred ten-thousands)

(2) Ten million: "Sen **man**" (one thousand ten-thousands)

(3) One hundred million: "**Oku**"

(1) One billion: "Juu **oku**" (ten one-hundred-millions)

Because Japanese is every four digits, many people also place the comma in English numerals after the fourth digit as well. Therefore, the number one billion would be written 10,0000,0000 instead of 1,000,000,000.

Shopping

Who doesn't buy at least a souvenir or two when traveling? As such, you may want to be familiar with some basic phrases for communication with shop attendants (see Table 14-10).

TABLE 14-10 Shopping

English	Japanese Script	Romanized Japanese
How much is this?	これはいくらですか	Kore wa ikura desu ka?
I'll take this please	これを下さい	Kore o kudasai

Restaurants

Next to navigating the train system, dining out may be one of the more difficult aspects of traveling in Japan. When you enter a restaurant, you may be asked a couple of questions, and if the waiter or waitress doesn't speak English, you may find yourself in a bit of a bind. Knowing common questions can help prevent that (see Table 14-11).

TABLE 14-11 Restaurants

English	Japanese Script	Romanized Japanese
Will you eat here or take out?	こちらで召し上がりますか?お持ち帰りですか?	Kochira de meshiagarimasu ka? omochikaeri desu ka?
I'm eating here	てんないで	Tennai de
I'm taking this to go	持ち帰りで	Mochikaeri de
How many people?	何名様ですか	Nan mei sama desu ka?
Nonsmoking table please	禁煙お願いします	Kin'en onegaishimasu
Smoking table please	喫煙席お願いします	Kitsuenseki onegaishimasu
Please sit here	こちらへどうぞ	Kochira e douzo
Do you have an English menu?	英語のメニューがあります	Eigo no menyuu ga arimasu ka?
Do you have a vegetarian menu?	ベジタリアンメニューがありますか	Bejitarian menyuu ga arimasu ka?
I am allergic to [*food item*]	[*Food item*]にアレルギーがあります	[*Food item*] ni arerugi ga arimasu
I'll have [*menu item*]	[*Menu item*]お願いします	[*Menu item*] onegaishimasu
What do you recommend?	おすすめは何ですか	Osusume wa nan desu ka?

English	Japanese Script	Romanized Japanese
Thanks for the food! I'm ready to eat!	いただきます	Itadakimasu
Thanks for the food! The food was delicious!	ごちそうさまでした	Gochisousama deshita

REMEMBER

If you have any dietary restrictions or important allergies, you'll want to make sure to commit these phrases to memory or have this book handy so you can inform the staff right away.

In the United States, smoking indoors is prohibited. However, that's not the case in Japan. Therefore, when visiting restaurants, you'll likely still be asked whether you want to be seating in a smoking or nonsmoking section.

Lastly, you may hear people say both *itadakimasu* and *gochisousama deshita*. Both are commonly translated as "Thanks for the food." However, *itadakimasu* is typically said before beginning to eat, and *gochisousama deshita* is said when you're done eating.

Conversations

Communicating with people in a foreign language can be difficult. Everybody speaks just a little bit differently. I personally found men harder to understand than women. In the case that you're having trouble understanding someone, you'll want to be able to let him know (see Table 14-12).

TABLE 14-12 Conversations

English	Japanese Script	Romanized Japanese
I don't understand Japanese	日本語が分かりません	Nihongo ga wakarimasen
I don't understand	分かりません	Wakarimasen
Can you repeat that? One more time please?	もう一度お願いします	Mou ichido onegaishimasu
Can you please speak slower?	ゆっくり話して下さい	Yukkuri hanashite kudasai
Do you speak English?	英語が話せますか	Eigo ga hanasemasu ka?

Other useful phrases

In Table 14-13, I list a few more words and phrases that are worth committing to memory. If you need to find a restroom or don't feel well and need to go to the hospital, having these memorized instead of needing to look them up can be incredibly helpful.

Also, be aware that some places may ask you to remove your shoes before entering. You can learn more about this custom in Chapter 16.

TABLE 14-13 Other Useful Words and Phrases

English	Japanese Script	Romanized Japanese
Where is the restroom?	トイレはどこですか	Toire wa doko desu ka?
I don't feel well	気分が悪いです	Kibun ga warui desu
Hospital	病院	Byouin

Chapter **15**

Getting Around Tokyo

I f you're somebody who lives in a big city, such as New York, maybe you won't find Japan's transportation system too intimidating. However, as somebody who grew up in the suburbs and had never really ridden a train before, I found the transportation system to be a little overwhelming. Looking back, I likely would have found it pretty easy if I had just done a bit of research beforehand in order to know what to expect.

This chapter is designed to do just that for you, so you'll be an absolute pro and leave all your friends and family wondering how you know so much!

Looking at the Modes of Transit in Japan

There are four main ways to get around Japan: public transit (including trains and local buses), highway buses, a rental car, and taxis and ride shares. During the Olympics, the Tokyo Organizing Committee of the Olympic and Paralympic Games recommends using public transit in order to get between the venues (Chapter 5) and your accommodations (Chapter 10). For that reason, this chapter primarily focuses on public transit. However, if you travel outside of Tokyo to do some exploring, you may find the other methods of transit useful.

Public transit: Trains and local buses

In large cities, such as Tokyo and Osaka, trains and subways serve as the primary mode of transportation. Local buses in these areas serve as the secondary method of transit and often extend the train and subway networks. In other less dense cities and rural areas, buses serve as the primary method of transit.

Japan's public transit system is incredibly extensive and allows travelers to get most places they want to go with ease. However, its size can also be a bit intimidating. More details about how to navigate this extremely useful but somewhat intimidating system are found in the following "Navigating the Train System" and "Riding the Bus" sections.

Highway buses

Highway buses are popular for long-distance travel. They're slower than other methods of transit, such as the bullet train, but they're often much cheaper (unless you have a Japan Rail Pass — more on this in the "Understanding the various types of train passes" section).

I use a highway bus when going long distances because then I have the option to take an overnight bus. That means I don't have to spend valuable daylight hours traveling. Plus, it's one less night I have to pay for a hotel. However, highway buses are definitely not as comfortable as hotel beds, so it's a tradeoff.

TIP

Personally, the only time I would choose to use a highway bus over the bullet train is if I were traveling a long distance and didn't have a Japan Rail Pass.

TIP

If you opt to take a highway bus, I recommend Willer Express. I use them for all my overnight travel and even some day travel. I've had fantastic experiences with them, and they travel to most major destinations in Japan.

REMEMBER

Note that most, if not all, highway buses require advance reservation and typically do not accept IC Cards as payment, like local buses do. Willer Express accepts credit cards, as well as payments at local convenience stores, such as Lawson and Family Mart. If possible, I recommend making reservations as far in advance as possible, because there will likely be many people traveling around the time of the Olympics.

If you plan on using highway buses frequently, you may also want to look into the Japan Bus Pass. You can purchase a three-day, five-day, or seven-day version of the pass that can be used on up to three Willer Express operated buses per day.

Rental cars

In order to be able to rent a car in Japan, you'll need to obtain an International Driving Permit (IDP) or Japanese driving license. You can't drive in Japan with just your U.S. driver's license.

The IDP is a translation of your personal information, including your driving information, into ten different languages. Unless you plan on moving to Japan, an IDP will suffice for your driving needs.

TIP

Most IDPs are valid for one year. If you already have an IDP, make sure yours will be valid for the duration of your trip to Japan.

WARNING

If you are considering renting a car in Japan, you must obtain your IDP before departing for Japan, because you won't be able to obtain an IDP while in Japan (unless you can afford to wait four to six weeks for AAA to ship one to you).

Lastly, you must be at least 18 years old to be able to drive in Japan.

If you're 18 and you have your IDP, you're ready to rent your car. Popular car rental companies in Japan include:

>> **Ekiren:** www.ekiren.co.jp/phpapp/en

>> **Nippon Rentacar:** www.nrgroup-global.com/en

>> **Nissan Rentacar:** https://nissan-rentacar.com/english

>> **Orix Rentacar:** https://car.orix.co.jp/eng

>> **Times Car Rental:** www.timescar-rental.com/en

>> **Toyota Rentacar:** https://rent.toyota.co.jp/eng

Other car rental companies you may be familiar with (including Alamo, Budget, Enterprise, National, and others) also have services in Japan but may or may not be more expensive than the top rental car companies in Japan.

Taxis and ride shares

Not so fun fact: Using private vehicles for ride sharing is prohibited by law in Japan. However, that doesn't mean that popular ride-sharing services such as Uber don't exist in Japan. In fact, Uber does offer services in Japan, but it has partnered with local taxi companies in order to be able to do so.

That said, Uber is not as popular in Japan as it is in the United States, and it may not necessarily be the cheapest option.

TIP

In Japan, taxis are still a very popular method of travel in areas where public transit is infrequent or unavailable. You can hail them from the side of the road or find them at taxi stands (usually located in front of train stations). Although it may be counterintuitive, a red light on the dash of the car indicates that the taxi is vacant and available for rides, and a green light indicates that the car is occupied.

Be aware that the left-rear door of the taxi door can be opened and closed remotely by the driver, so you're not supposed to open or close the door of a taxi unless you're using another one of the doors (the passenger door or right-rear door). Don't be taken by surprise if the door automatically swings open as the taxi comes to a stop in front of you.

Fares vary depend on the location where you're catching the taxi and the size of the taxi. However, there is usually a flat fee for the first kilometer or two (a little over a mile). The fee then increases approximately every 300 meters (0.18 mile). There is also a waiting fare if the taxi has to slow down or stop for heavy traffic, for example. Lastly, if the taxi must travel by highway, any incurred highway fees (think toll roads) will be added to your fare.

Not all taxis accept credit cards, and some may not have cash for large bills such as the ¥10,000 ($91.74), so it's always best to keep some small bills of cash with you. Some taxis now also accept IC Cards. (See Chapter 13 for more information on cash and payment methods in Japan.)

WARNING

Finding the Best Route

Sometimes the best way to get from point A to point B can involve walking, riding the train, or taking the bus . . . or it can utilize all three. Thankfully, many websites and mobile apps make figuring out how to get from point A to point B relatively easy. I can't even imagine trying to read a physical map of Tokyo.

Google Maps and Apple's own Maps app are the go-to apps for most people. They do a pretty good job of figuring out the best route and present it in an easy-to-follow format.

TIP

However, I actually prefer an app called Japan Travel – route, map, JR on iOS and Japan Travel – route, map, JR, taxi, Wi-fi on Android (catchy names, I know, but if you search in the app store for your phone, you'll find it). It shows the names of train stations in both English and Japanese, which can be useful when asking for directions. Plus, it gives you the option to prioritize train routes operated by the Japan Rail Company, which is useful if you have a Japan Rail Pass you're trying to take full advantage of (more on the Japan Rail Pass in the following sections).

TIP

Many other frequent Japan travelers recommend Hyperdia and Japan Transit Planner, both of which offer similar features, such as optimizing for the Japan Rail Pass.

The only downfall to the Japan Travel, Hyperdia, and Japan Transit Planner apps is that they mostly only recognize train stations and popular tourist attractions as points of departure and arrival. If you're trying to find the nearest train station to your hotel, they won't be of much help.

Navigating the Train System

Japan's train system is incredibly extensive, making it super convenient for getting around. However, it also has a few layers of complexity that can make it a bit intimidating to first-time riders. However, when you know what to expect, getting around becomes a breeze!

Finding the correct rail company

There are several different *railway operators* (companies that operate rail lines in Japan). Approximately 70 percent of the rail lines in Japan are owned and operated by the Japan Railways (JR) Group. The rest of the rail lines are owned and operated by other private railway companies.

Sometimes, one station can have railways from multiple different rail companies running through it. For example, Ikebukuro Station located in Ikebukuro (one of the areas within Tokyo) has rail lines from four different companies: JR, Seibu Railway, Tobu Railway, and Tokyo Metro.

Thankfully, all the rail lines are grouped together in a station based on what company they're operated by. So, if your GPS is telling you to get on the JR Yamanote line at Ikebukuro Station, you first need to locate the JR section of Ikebukuro station.

Most major stations, especially in Tokyo, have signs that are written in both Japanese and English, and there are plenty of signs. It should be relatively easy to locate the rail company you're looking for. However, if you can't find it, don't be afraid to ask a staff member. I *lived* in Tokyo and still couldn't find my way around Shinjuku Station, so don't feel bad about asking. Most of the apps mentioned in the "Finding the Best Route" section will also tell you where to enter and exit the train station (because most stations have multiple entrances) to help you enter the station as close to the correct rail company as possible.

Paying for your ride

In order to enter one of the railway company sections within a train station, you have to go through a set of gates. Before you can go through the gates, though, you need to pay for your train ride.

There are a few different ways to pay for your ride: a traditional ticket, an IC Card, or a train pass. Depending on how you decide to spend your time in Japan, you may only ever use one of these payment methods, or you may use all three.

Buying a ticket for the train

I only recommend buying physical train tickets if you absolutely must. IC Cards and train passes (which I cover in the next sections) are way more convenient and will likely even save you money. However, if you misplace your IC Card or train pass, or maybe your train pass hasn't been activated yet, you may find yourself having to buy a physical ticket, so it's important to understand how it works.

First, know that train ticket kiosks are specific to the railway company at which they're stationed. Going back to my previous example, if you're in Ikebukuro Station and you want to ride the JR Yamanote line, you can't buy a train ticket at the kiosks located at the Tobu Railway, Seibu Railway, and so on. You can only buy a ticket for the JR Yamanote line from a JR kiosk.

Most railway companies have a map of their various rail lines above the kiosks. I highly suggest looking at this map before you actually get in line for the kiosk, because you'll need the information on it to figure out what kind of ticket you need to buy.

Train fares are based on total distance traveled. This means that you could ride the train all day, but you'd only be charged for the absolute distance traveled, not the total distance you traveled for the duration of the day. I can't think of anybody who would actually want to just sit on a train all day, but this fact becomes important in case you accidentally get off at the wrong stop (more on this in the "Knowing what to do if you get on the wrong train or off at the wrong stop" section, later in this chapter).

When you look at the map, you'll want to locate the rail line you intend on riding. At Ikebukuro Station, there are three different JR lines: the Yamanote line, the Saikyō line, and the Shōnan-Shinjuku line. For the example I'm using, you'd want to locate the Yamanote line on the map.

For each line, the map will have a "You Are Here" indicator, as well as a list of all the stops along the line. Some of the more popular stops along the route may even be emphasized, allowing you to locate them more easily. Next to the name of each stop, you also see the amount it costs to ride there.

Figure 15-1 is a map of the JR Yamanote line. The Yamanote line is unique in that the line runs in a circle (which is a bit unusual for a rail line in Japan). The You Are Here indicator shows that you're at Ikebukuro Station. If you wanted to go to Shinjuku Station, it would cost ¥160 ($1.47). If you wanted to go to Akihabara Station, it would cost ¥200 ($1.83).

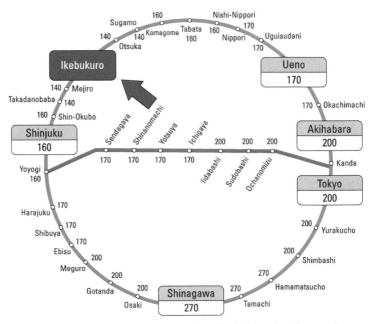

FIGURE 15-1: A map of the JR Yamanote line displaying prices for traveling to each of the stops from Ikebukuro Station.

REMEMBER

When you locate the station where you want to get off, make a note of the cost. You'll need this number when you go to buy a ticket.

When you walk up to the kiosk, look for a Language button or English button. Pressing this button will allow you to change the instructions on the screen to English. Convenient, right? On rare occasions, if you're in the more rural parts of Japan, you may run into a kiosk that doesn't offer instructions in English. In this case, your best bet is to ask a staff member (assuming you can't read Japanese).

When the screen is in English, you'll find that you have a couple of different options. To buy a single train ride ticket, you'll want to press the Ticket button. Then select the price amount (the number you found on the map earlier). You also have the option to select the quantity of tickets you want to purchase. Then put your money into the machine, and it will spit out your train ticket.

Using an IC Card

IC Cards are reloadable smart cards. You can load money onto the IC Card and then use it to pay for your train and bus rides. The fare of your train ride will automatically be calculated and deducted from your IC Card when you exit the gate. It makes riding the train much more convenient because you don't have to look at a map, figure out where you're going, and calculate how much it costs. Of course, you need enough money on your card to cover your fare, so it's a good idea to have at least a rough estimate of what your fare will cost.

TIP

Even if you purchase a train pass (see the next section), you'll likely still want an IC Card to use on the train lines that aren't covered by your train pass.

You can purchase IC Cards at the same ticket kiosks you would use to buy traditional train tickets.

It's important to note that there are several different IC Card brands, such as Icoca, Pasmo, Suica, and Toica. However, all IC Cards brands are accepted by any train station or bus route that accepts IC Cards as a form of payment, so you don't have to worry about what brand of IC Card you buy.

REMEMBER

The only important thing to note is that if you want to get your money back off the card (for example, when you're getting ready to leave Japan), you have to return the IC Card to the same company you received it from. For example, if you purchase an IC Card from one of the non-JR companies in Ikebukuro Station (Seibu Railway, Tobu Railway, or Tokyo Metro), you'll receive a Pasmo Card. When you go to leave Japan, you need to return your Pasmo card to the same issuer (Pasmo cards are issued by all the non-JR companies in the greater Tokyo area). You won't be able to return your Pasmo card at a station in Osaka, for example.

When you walk up to the kiosk, instead of selecting Ticket, look for a button that has one of the IC Card brands. In Tokyo, this would be either Suica (issued by JR lines) or Pasmo (issued by non-JR lines). You'll then see a Purchase New PASMO button (or something similar).

You may be given the option to select a blank or personalized version of your IC Card. Personalized cards require you to register your card with your name, gender, date of birth, and phone number.

TIP

The benefit of a personalized card is that it can be reissued if you happen to lose it. Blank cards cannot. However, there is often paperwork and a fee associated with getting an IC Card reissued, and it's likely only worth it if you keep a high balance on your card. In my opinion, you're better off just going with a blank card and not keeping a ridiculously high balance on the card. However, some people think the personalized card makes for a good souvenir, so it's up to you.

Next, you'll be asked to select how much money you would like to load onto the card. Keep in mind that there is a deposit of ¥500 ($4.59) for the card itself (which you get back when you return the card), so if you choose the ¥2,000 ($18.35) option, ¥500 ($4.59) will be used to cover the deposit and ¥1,500 ($13.76) will be loaded onto the card for you to start using.

Some train stations have begun offering IC Cards specifically for tourists. These IC Cards don't have the ¥500 ($4.59) deposit, but they're only valid for 28 days.

After you've selected the amount you want, enter the money into the machine, and then the kiosk will dispense your brand-new card!

After you've used up your balance, you can return to a ticket kiosk to add more funds to your card. Simply walk up to any train station ticket kiosk (it doesn't have to be the same brand that issued your card) and insert your IC Card. The machine will display your current balance and a list of options for how much you want to add to the card. After you select the amount you want to add, insert the appropriate amount of cash, and the machine will return the card to you with the updated balance.

Understanding the various types of train passes

Train passes typically allow you to pay a flat fee and then ride certain rail lines an unlimited number of times for a set duration of time.

The most common is the Japan Rail Pass, often shortened to just JR Pass. It comes in three different versions: 7-day, 14-day, and 21-day. It lets you ride any JR-operated train, bus, or ferry (yes, Japan Railway operates more than trains) an unlimited number of times for the length of time you chose. The keyword here is *any*. This is one of the only train passes that will work nationwide. It's also one of the only passes that can be used on some of the bullet trains.

There are also more specialized train passes, limited to specific areas of Japan. For example, the JR Tokyo Wide Pass allows for unlimited travel in the Greater Tokyo area on all JR trains and some non-JR trains for up to three days. The Tokyo Subway Ticket allows unlimited travel on the Tokyo Metro rail lines for 24 hours, 48 hours, or 72 hours, depending on the type of pass you purchase. Other area-specific passes include the Nikko Pass and the Hakone Kamakura Pass, which provide unlimited travel on trains in the Nikko area and Kamakura area, respectively, for a set amount of time. It may be worth picking up these passes if you plan on taking a few day trips from Tokyo (more on day trips in Chapter 17).

If you decide to purchase a train pass, know that train passes work a little differently from tickets and IC Cards. You can't go through the automated turnstile gates. Instead, there will be a staff member stationed near the gates, usually inside a glass box. Show the staff member your train pass, and he'll let you through.

Deciding whether the train passes are worth it

When used effectively, train passes can save you a significant amount of money. However, if you don't use them to the max, you end up not getting your money's worth. Before buying a train pass, it's worth looking at what you have planned for your trip to see whether it will be worth the money spent.

For example, if you just plan on visiting Tokyo for the first week of the Olympics, you may be tempted to buy the seven-day JR Pass. However, as of this writing, the seven-day JR Pass costs $275.

Given that a ride of the previously mentioned JR Yamanote line typically costs anywhere from $1.50 to $2 per ride, you'd have to ride the train approximately 147 times in order to get your money's worth! Assuming you take the train from your hotel to two different Olympic venues and then back to your hotel, you'd only be riding the train three or four times a day, totaling about 56 times for the week — only half of what you'd need to get your money's worth from the JR Pass.

Unless you plan on doing a *crazy* amount of travel within Tokyo, the JR Pass usually only saves money for those who plan on taking longer trips to other parts of the country. If you start thinking about visiting other popular destinations in Japan such as Kyoto or Hiroshima, then the JR Pass starts becoming more useful.

TIP

For more examples of when the JR Pass is and is not worth it, you can check out this post on my blog: https://footstep sofadreamer.com/japan-rail-pass-jr-pass-worth-it.

The Tokyo Subway Ticket, on the other hand, may be worth it, especially if your hotels and the venues you plan on visiting are near some of the Tokyo Metro stations.

Using the same example from earlier, let's assume you plan on taking the subway from your hotel to two different Olympic venues and then back to your hotel. Depending on how far your hotel and the venues are, you could pay up to $2.50 per ride for a total of $7.50 for the day. If you do that for three days, your total would be $22.50. However, the 72-hour Tokyo Subway Ticket is, at the time of this writing, approximately $15, so you'd save $7.50, and that's assuming you don't do any additional sightseeing or exploring.

Riding the train

After you've paid for your ride, you can finally ride the train, but sometimes that's the scary part. You have to make sure you get on the right train, get off at the right stop, and not accidentally annoy anybody along the way. However, if you can keep the next few paragraphs in mind, you'll be golden.

Japan-guide.com has also put together a nice video of this process. You can find it at www.youtube.com/watch?v=aW_sw77sqvE.

Going through the gates

After you have your ticket, or if you plan to use an IC Card, you'll want to head to the gates for the appropriate railway company. For example, if you're planning on riding the JR Yamanote line, you'll want to make sure that you're at the JR gates.

Most gates have some sort of indicator as to which ones you can enter through. Most times they either have a green arrow or are lit up with a blue light if you can enter. If you see a red X or the gate is lit up red, it means that you can't enter through that gate. If you can't enter through a particular gate, it's usually because that gate is reserved for those who are exiting. This helps keep traffic in the stations flowing without people running into each other.

If you're using a ticket, there will be a slot for you to input the ticket. Most times, there is a yellow box around the ticket slot so you can easily see it. After you input the ticket into the machine, you'll be able to walk through the gate, and your ticket will pop out on the top of the gate at the end.

REMEMBER

Remember to grab your train ticket after you walk through the gate. You need it later to get out of the station after you arrive at your destination.

If you're using your IC Card, look for an IC Card reader on the right hand side of the gate. Touch your IC Card to the reader, and it will beep, letting you know that you can go through the gate. The screen will also display the balance on your card so you can double-check that you have enough to pay for your ride.

TIP

If you don't have enough money loaded onto your card, there are machines inside the gates that you can use to load more money onto your IC Card.

Also, keep in mind that the train stations can be super busy. In order to help keep things moving, it's best to only walk up to the gates if you have your ticket or IC Card ready to go. Don't stand in front of the gate and then try to dig through your bag for your IC Card. Instead, stand off to the side or along the wall until you're able to locate your card or ticket.

TIP

Many people keep their IC Cards in their phones or wallets or even in card holders attached to their bags for easy access. Most people can just hold their phones or wallets to the IC Card reader without having to actually get their IC Cards out and get through the gates without a problem.

Getting on the right train

At the gate and even inside the gates there will be signs overhead with a list of rail lines and the platform number that services those rail lines.

Some rail companies have only one rail line option, making finding the platform you need relatively easy. One platform will have trains heading in one direction. The second platform will have trains heading in the other directions.

However, bigger railway companies (such as JR) often have multiple rail lines. For example, from the Ikebukuro Station you can ride the JR Shōnan-Shinjuku line, JR Saikyō line, and the JR Yamanote line. In this case, you first need to locate the correct rail line, and then determine which direction you need to be heading.

For example, if you're at Ikebukuro Station, the trains on the JR Yamanote line bound for the Shinjuku or Shibuya area (heading counterclockwise on the circuit) arrive and depart from platforms 5 and 6. Trains heading in the clockwise direction toward Ueno depart and arrive at platforms 7 and 8.

If you use an app or travel website such as Hyperdia or Japan Transit Planner, it may tell you the platform you need.

TIP If you're ever confused about which platform you need to go to, don't hesitate to ask a local staff member. If you tell them what station you would like to go to, they'll direct you toward the correct platform.

When you arrive at your platform, there will be an electronic sign overhead showing arriving trains. It will display the time the train is estimated to arrive, the type of train it is (more on this in the next paragraph), and the last station it will stop at. At most stations, these signs will rotate between Japanese and English.

There are three main types of trains: local, rapid (sometimes called semi-express), and express. Local trains stop at every station. Rapid or semi-express trains stop at most stations but skip some of the smaller stations. Express trains typically stop only at some of the bigger stations.

In most stations, there will be posters on the wall displaying which types of trains stop at which stations. This way, you can ensure that you get on a train that will be stopping at your destination.

TIP

There are spots on the ground indicating where the doors on the train will be when the train arrives. This will be where the line to board the train begins.

At many stations, when the train is close to arriving, there will be an announcement over the PA systems. Sometimes it's announced in both Japanese and English, but not always. In general, the announcement is usually something along the lines of, "Soon, on [number] platform, [type of train] bound for [final destination] will be arriving. For your safety, please stay behind the yellow line."

After the train arrives at the station, it's common courtesy for people who are standing in line at the platform to step to the side of the train door so that people exiting the train have a clear path to get off. Only after everybody is done exiting the train do the people in line on the platform begin boarding.

WARNING

Be aware that certain train lines can be very, very crowded during certain parts of the day. I remember standing on a station platform watching people board a train and thinking, "There's no way any more people can fit on that train." Then, sure enough, a few more people would squeeze their way on. Then even more people would squeeze their way on! If you haven't already seen videos of this, I suggest searching "Japan crowded trains" on YouTube. Some of those videos showcase the more extreme examples, but they're not far off from what you might encounter.

During the Olympics, the trains will likely be even more crowded than usual. Don't be surprised if you end up shoulder to shoulder with several people (or, if you're short like me, with your face in somebody's back). There were times where I definitely felt like a sardine packed in so tight, I couldn't even move an inch. Thankfully, though, I found that there are a few tips that can help you avoid these situations.

TIP

If the train is packed, I recommend trying to be either the first one on the train or the last person on the train. The first person onto the train can usually go farther into the train, toward the middle (the area between the two door entrances). This area tends to be less crowded. The last person on the train will have the door next to them. In this case, your back will likely be pressed against somebody behind you, but you won't have anybody in front of you, giving you some space to breathe.

Remembering train etiquette

TIP

Given how crowded trains and Tokyo in general can be, keeping a few train etiquette points in mind can help ensure that you don't annoy others:

>> **Take off backpacks and large bags.** Many trains have shelves that run along the top on both sides where you can store bags. Otherwise, keeping your bag in front of you or on the floor in between your legs will keep it from bumping into others.

>> **Avoid talking on the phone.** Talking on the phone is typically seen as a disturbance to other passengers and is, thus, viewed as being rude. Similarly, keep headphone volume low enough that the person next to you can't hear, and if you're traveling with companions, keep your voices low when you talk.

>> **Refrain from eating and drinking.** You may see food and drinks on long-distance train rides (such as bullet trains across the country), but eating and drinking are considered to be inappropriate on regular trains.

>> **Respect priority seating.** Certain spots on each train car are dedicated to the elderly, those who have health problems, and those who are pregnant or have small children with them. If there are no passengers who meet this criteria, feel free to sit in these seats. However, be ready to get up and offer it to somebody who needs it. They may not always accept it, but at least offer it.

Getting off the train

Many trains have a scrolling announcement bar or a light-up map to indicate which stop is coming up next. These will typically be displayed in Japanese first and then in English. In addition, there will almost always be an announcement in Japanese about the next stop. Announcements in English are common on trains in bigger cities, but they're less common in less-touristy areas.

Unlike some of the public transit systems in the United States, the announcements are typically quite loud. Most of them are also automated, so you don't have to worry about not being able to hear the announcement.

Many people who plan to get off at the next stop make their way toward the door as they near their stop, but it's not absolutely necessary. It just makes for a smoother and quicker transition, because most people will wait to start boarding until everybody who intends to get off has done so.

Knowing what to do if you get on the wrong train or off at the wrong stop

So, what happens if you get off at the wrong stop? Or worse, maybe you got on the wrong train to begin with!

TIP

The best part of the Japanese train system is that you're only charged for the distance traveled between your departing station and arriving station. You're not charged for how far you actually ride the train. This means that if you get on the wrong train or get off at the wrong stop, as long as you don't go through the exit gates (to exit out of the particular railway company and into the regular train station), you can get back on the train and head in the right direction without having to pay more money.

If you do happen to get off at the wrong stop or get on the wrong train, try not to stress out about it. In bigger cities such as Tokyo, trains run quite frequently, which means it won't be long before another train comes by. Being able to laugh at yourself will be instrumental in ensuring that you have a good trip. During my travel mishaps, of which I've had many, I always tell myself, "It's a new adventure! Let's see where it leads."

Going out of the gates

Going out of the gates is much like entering the gates. After you get off the train, you'll exit the platform and find yourself standing at the gates. You'll want to make sure you either have your ticket or IC Card ready to go.

If you used a ticket to ride the train, you'll insert the ticket into the slot, similar to how you did when entering the gates. You'll be able to then exit out of the gate. However, this time the ticket won't pop up at the end. The machine will just eat the ticket because you've completed your ride.

If you used an IC Card to enter the gates, you'll also use it to exit. Hold your card up to the IC Card reader, and it will beep after it has registered your card. It will display the amount you were charged, as well as the new balance on your card, and then you're free to pass through the gate. If for some reason you don't have enough money on your IC Card to cover your fare, the gates will typically flash red. There are typically ticket kiosks near the exit gates where you can load more money onto your IC Card and then try again to exit.

Other things to know about riding the train

One of the things many foreigners find fascinating when visiting Japan is the way many Japanese can fall asleep, and I mean truly be fast asleep, and then magically wake up when it's time to get off the train. Most people who fall asleep on the train typically drop their heads forward or back against the window so as not to disturb others. However, every now and then somebody will accidentally fall asleep on the shoulder of the person next to him. That's generally considered somewhat rude (unless the person is your friend), but don't be surprised if it happens to you.

WARNING

Having someone fall asleep on your shoulder is one thing, but on occasion, women experience more extreme problems. Groping or sexual molestation on public trains has been a problem in Japan for a long time and even has its own term in Japanese: *chikan.* It happens frequently enough that some train lines even have specific train cars that are women only, particularly during rush hour. Don't let this scare you from taking the train, but keep it in the back of your mind and always be vigilant.

If you do have an encounter with a *chikan,* speak up! Make a scene! Many people are often too stunned or in disbelief to think to say something. Regardless of your initial reaction, make sure to report the incident to the first staff member you see. If you had the wherewithal to call the person out on it, you can even drag the person with you to the station official.

Riding the Bus

The bus system can be a little confusing, if only because it seems to vary depending on where you are.

In Tokyo

In Tokyo, buses are typically a flat fee, which varies by what route you take. You enter through the front door and pay for your fare when you enter. This can either be done with cash or with an IC Card. If you don't have exact change for the bus fare, there is usually a coin machine located at the front of the bus to get change.

An electronic display at the front of the bus will display what stop is coming up next, and a button located along the wall of the bus or sometimes even on the railings allows you to indicate to the driver that you'd like to get off at the next stop. For the Tokyo buses, you typically exit out the back door (it's called the back door, but it's usually in the middle of the bus).

Outside Tokyo

Outside Tokyo, things work a bit differently. Fares are typically calculated by distance traveled (unless you're in Kyoto, which also has a flat-rate system). For this reason, you typically board the bus in the back, not the front. If you plan to pay by cash, grab a ticket from the ticket machine near the door. If you want to use your IC Card, tap your IC Card to the reader near the back entrance.

Like the Tokyo buses, other buses around Japan have a button that you can use to indicate to the driver when you want to stop. However, the display board will likely look a bit different from the Tokyo buses. The display boards for these buses also display the prices for each stop, depending on where you boarded the bus.

When you go to get off at your stop, head to the front of the bus. If you got onto the bus using your IC Card, tap your IC Card to the reader near the front door, and then you're free to exit. If you took a ticket, you'll want to insert your ticket into the fare box and then insert the exact change before exiting the bus.

Chapter **16**

Fitting In: Customs, Manners, and Laws

I f you've never been to Japan, or Asia in general, you'll most likely experience a bit of culture shock. The Japanese way of life isn't terribly different from the English-speaking world, but there are enough differences to take you out of your comfort zone. Knowing the differences can help make the transition smoother and ensure you don't embarrass yourself or get yourself into trouble.

Staying to the Left

When you go up the steps, which side of the steps do you stay on? When you walk down the sidewalk, which part of the sidewalk do you usually walk on?

Did you by chance answer the right side? If you live in a country where people drive on the right side of the road, you probably also tend to stay to the right when you're walking.

In Japan, driving and walking are done on the left side. As an American, this took me a while to adjust to because it was my habit to stay on the right. Sometimes I would do it without thinking and then find myself facing a sea of oncoming people because I was standing on the wrong side of the sidewalk.

The same also applies to escalators. If you plan to stand on an escalator, make sure to stand on the left side. This keeps the right side clear for people who want to walk up or down the escalator.

WARNING

The exception to this rule is when you're in the Osaka and Kyoto area (approximately four hours west of Tokyo by bullet train). For whatever reason, people who live in this area stand on the right side of the escalator while keeping the left side clear for those who want to walk up it.

TIP

Don't worry if you can't remember which part of Japan walks on which side of the stairs. When in Japan, do as the Japanese do, and just follow what everybody around you is doing.

Removing Your Shoes

If you go over to a friend's house, do you typically remove your shoes inside the doorway before entering the rest of the house? Depending on your own habits, and your friend's preferences, you may or may not leave your shoes on.

In Japan, removing your shoes when entering somebody's home or apartment is much more important than it sometimes is in the rest of the world. Historically, Japanese people often slept and even ate on the floor, so it was very important for the floors to be clean. Thus, removing shoes was a must. Even though most Japanese people have Western-style dinner tables and beds now, they still take off their shoes before entering the house.

The likelihood of your entering somebody's home during your time in Japan is probably pretty slim (unless you have friends in the area). However, depending on what kind of hotel or apartment you stay in, you may be asked to remove your shoes before entering. You'll most likely be given slippers to put on. On the off chance that you aren't given slippers, just walk around in your socks or go barefoot. If you have to use the restroom while visiting, you'll find a separate pair of slippers to slip on while in the restroom. Just make sure to put on your original pair of slippers again when you exit the restroom and leave the toilet slippers for the next person using the restroom.

You may also encounter this custom when visiting various places of cultural significance, such as shrines and temples. I was also occasionally asked to remove my shoes before entering dressing rooms at clothing stores.

Being Considerate of Others

Given Japan's very dense population, especially in bigger cities like Tokyo, things can be quite crowded. Most Japanese people are very aware of the fact that many actions they take will have a direct impact on those around them.

Japanese society, in general, has a very group-oriented way of thinking, as opposed to other countries, such as the United States, where people have a more individualist mentality. As such, Japanese people generally will go to great lengths to avoid irritating others. They don't play music very loud and people refrain from talking on the train (whether to traveling companions or on the phone). That's not to say that one way of thinking is better than another (all societies have their issues), but it's something to keep in mind while in Japan.

TIP

In general, I recommend making more of an effort than you may normally to stay aware of your surroundings and be cognizant of how your actions may be affecting those around you.

Keeping Germs to Yourself

In the Western world, if people are sick, they tend to keep to themselves. They may do their best to avoid coming into contact with others, such as shaking somebody's hand. However, because of how crowded cities are, this can be very hard to do in Japan. As such, you often see people wear surgical masks to help prevent others from getting sick. You also see healthy people wear them in an effort to avoid getting sick themselves.

Navigating Food and Restaurants

When it comes to eating and dining in Japan, a couple of practices exist in Japan that don't exist in the West. The opposite of that statement is also true. Some customs that exist in the West aren't present in Japan. Knowing these customs can ensure you don't accidentally offend someone.

Eating inside (not out)

In the United States, I have a habit of sort of eating on the go. I pick up food and eat it on the way to my next destination. However, in general, in Japan, it's typically considered impolite to eat while walking down the street or riding on the train. If you order something to go, wait until you get back to your hotel to eat it or find a park bench or seating area to stop at before digging into your food. Many convenience stores that sell food will also have a seating area inside the store for you to sit and eat at.

Using chopsticks

Most restaurants have silverware on hand if you aren't skilled with chopsticks, but I think it's worth at least giving them a shot.

WARNING

If you do decide to use chopsticks, here are just a couple things to keep in mind:

>> **Don't stick your chopsticks vertically into a bowl of rice.**
When not actively eating your rice, lay your chopsticks on top of the bowl, or set them on top of your napkin. Don't just leave them in your rice standing upright.

>> **Don't use chopsticks to pass food to another person.**
If you would like to give food to another person, place the food on the person's plate instead of passing from your chopsticks to their chopsticks.

Both of these actions are typically done during funerals and are, thus, considered taboo. Many people also believe that doing either of these things will bring bad luck.

Calling a server

At restaurants in the English-speaking world, waiters and waitresses typically stop by your table every couple of minutes to make sure you're doing okay and ask if you need anything. That's typically not the case in Japan. Most servers will leave you in peace unless you specifically indicate that you need something.

TIP

If you want a server to stop by your table, just call out, "Sumimasen" (which means "Excuse me" in Japanese) to a nearby waiter or waitress. Some larger and chain restaurants will even have a call server button on the table.

Making changes to the menu

In Japan, it's common that what is on the menu is what you get. If the menu says a bowl of ramen comes with *tonkatsu* (pork cutlet), chopped green onions, seaweed, and an egg, that's what you get. People typically don't ask for substitutions. The only exception to this is in the event that you're allergic to something.

Tipping

Most people are typically excited to hear that tipping is not customary in Japan. Many Japanese people will actually be offended if you try to give them a tip. This not only applies to waiters and waitresses in restaurants, but to all services (such as hairdressers, tour guides, and other services you would commonly tip for).

Hiding Your Tattoos

Historically, in Japan, tattoos were often given to people who had committed crimes. Over time, tattoos began to be associated with *yakuza*, members of gangs or organized crime. As such, Japan has developed a sort of stigma against tattoos. Although tattoos are slowly becoming more accepted in Japan, especially for foreigners, you may still encounter some people who have a negative reaction.

In general, you likely won't run into any issues just walking down the street with visible tattoos (although you may get quite a few stares). However, you may have issues when trying to visit swimming pools, *onsen* (see the next section), and other public bathing facilities. Travelers with visible tattoos have also reported having trouble visiting *ryokan* (traditional Japanese inns), shrines and temples, and even some restaurants.

Many travelers with tattoos simply keep their tattoos covered. However, that's not exactly possible to do when you visit bathing facilities, especially *onsen,* where no clothing is allowed. In these cases, many travelers have reported being able to enter the bathing facilities if they covered their tattoos with waterproof bandages.

Visiting Onsen: Going Au Naturel in Japanese Hot Springs

The word *onsen* refers to Japanese hot springs. Sometimes these are naturally occurring hot springs due to the high volcanic activity in Japan; other times, they're artificially created.

Bathing is an important aspect of Japanese culture because it's seen not only as a way to physically clean the dirt and sweat from your body, but also as a way to cleanse your spirit and improve your health. As such, it's not surprising that visiting *onsen* is a very popular activity in Japan.

However, it's also one of the most intimidating aspects for foreigners for two reasons: It's communal, meaning you bathe with other people, and it's done completely naked. No clothes allowed. Don't worry though. Almost all *onsen* are separated by gender.

Don't let these points put you off. Not only can it be incredibly relaxing and enjoyable, but it's also a fantastic way to experience Japanese culture firsthand.

That being said, there are a few things to keep in mind when visiting *onsen* to ensure that you don't offend other *onsen* visitors or make them feel uncomfortable:

>> **Wash off before entering the *onsen*.** You shouldn't actually be dirty when you enter the *onsen*. *Onsen* are more of a place to relax. There will typically be a showering area where you can wash yourself before entering the *onsen*.

>> **Nothing other than your body enters the water of the *onsen*.** This refers to the fact that you can't wear clothes into *onsen,* but it also refers to towels. Some *onsen* provide small towels that you can take with you, but they aren't allowed to touch the water. As such, many people wear the small towels on top of their heads.

>> **Do not enter *onsen* with open wounds.** For hygiene reasons, don't enter the *onsen* if you have open wounds, sores, or anything else that could allow bodily fluids to enter the water.

>> **Keep your head above water.** Dunking your head underwater could contribute to the spread of germs and also increase your chances of catching something.

>> **Tie up long hair.** If you have long hair, put it up with a hair tie before entering the water. In some cases, I've seen people leave their hair down if they've washed it first, but in general I recommend putting it up and keeping it out of the water so you don't have to deal with it.

>> **Be modest when not in the water.** Don't stare. Most people will use the small towel to keep themselves covered as they move between the changing area, showering area, and *onsen*.

Using the Toilets

You would think that using a toilet would be pretty self-explanatory. However, there are a few different types of toilets in Japan that may catch you off guard.

High-tech toilets

First, Japan has some pretty fancy toilets. They look just like the toilets found in the United States but have some additional features. Usually, these toilets will have buttons on the side.

One is a seat warmer, keeping the toilet seat warm even when it's cooler outside. They also typically have a bidet built in, which will spray water up at you to clean you. Some even have sensors that will automatically lift the lid when you approach and have buttons to play soft music to mask any other sounds made when using the restroom.

Old-fashioned toilets

Despite many places in Japan having fancy, high-tech toilets, you may, unfortunately, still come across places that have squat toilets (basically fancy holes in the ground that you squat over when doing your business). Squat toilets are not exactly fun to use (and much less fun when wearing high heels), but when you've got to go. . . . I found that I typically ran into these toilets in public areas such as parks. Other places like train stations will sometimes have both regular toilets and squat toilets, with the door to the stall marking which one is which.

Dealing with Trash

I was a bit surprised to find that trash was a bit more complicated in Japan than I was used to in the United States, but when I committed a few rules to memory, it wasn't so bad.

Dealing with different types of trash

In the United States, some places just have trash cans. Others have trash cans and recycling bins. It's only been in recent years that some places have started adding more recycling options, but these are still few and far between.

In Japan, they tend to divide out their trash into multiple different categories. It gets even more complicated by the fact that different areas of Japan divide their trash a bit differently.

In Tokyo, there are three main categories:

>> **Combustible trash:** This is the standard trash you would likely think of. It includes most food wrappings and boxes and food waste.

>> **Non-combustible trash:** As the name implies, these are items that can't be burned. Examples include items made of glass or metal.

>> **Recyclable trash:** This category includes common recyclable items such as plastic bottles, aluminum cans, newspapers, and similar items.

Carrying your trash

The other thing to note is that it's not very common to see trash receptacles when you're out and about. In the United States, I typically find trash cans lining the streets of popular cities, as well as around public areas such as parks. However, this isn't the case in Japan. Most people hang onto their trash while they're out and about and throw it away when they get home.

5

Extending Your Trip

IN THIS PART . . .

Discover other great things to do just outside of Tokyo.

Find worthwhile adventures across the country.

Chapter **17**

Taking a Day Trip from Tokyo

Tthere's more to Japan than just Tokyo. Sure, the main reason you're going to Japan is to watch the 2020 Summer Olympics, so of course the bulk of your time in Japan will be spent in Tokyo. However, if you have a few days where you aren't attending any Olympic events, I highly recommend checking out some of the areas outside of Tokyo. There are several places just outside the city (see Figure 17-1) that make for amazing day trips!

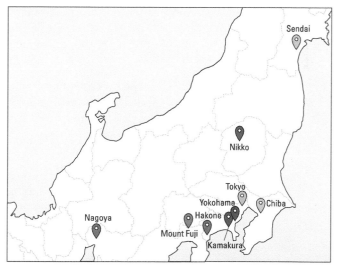

FIGURE 17-1: A map of popular day trips from Tokyo.

Nikko: A City Enshrined in History

I like to think of Nikko as "little Kyoto," although I'm probably the only one who calls it this (see Chapter 18 for more about Kyoto). Unlike Kyoto, it's not nearly as touristy, but it's just as rich in Japanese culture and history.

Nikko is probably most famous for its shrines and temples, which together make up a UNESCO World Heritage Site. The United Nations Educational, Scientific, and Cultural Organization (UNESCO) has identified these shrines and temples (as well as many other locations around the world) to be an integral part of the area's cultural and natural heritage and have outstanding value to humanity. As such, UNESCO works hard with other local communities and organizations to protect and preserve these important sites.

This UNESCO World Heritage Site primarily consists of Toshogu Shrine, Futarasan Jinja (Futarasan Shrine), and Rinno-ji Temple. Toshogu Shrine serves as the final resting place for Ieyasu Tokugawa, the founder of the Tokugawa Shogunate, the last feudal military government run by the Tokugawa family. With countless wood carvings and adornments, it's one of the more lavishly decorated shrines that you'll see in Japan. Futarasan Shrine is located right next to Toshogu Shrine and is dedicated to the deities of Nikko's three most sacred mountains: Mount Nantai, Mount Nyoho, and Mount Taro. Rinno-ji is famous for its three gold lacquered wooden statues that depict what are considered to be the manifestations of Futarasan's three mountain spirits. Also just behind Rinno-ji Temple is Shoyoen, a small but serene Japanese garden.

Also in Nikko is Taiyuinbyo, the mausoleum for Iemitsu Tokugawan, the third Tokugawa *shogun* (government head) and the grandson of Ieyasu. Here you'll find that the decorum is similar to that of Toshogu Shrine and contains both a prayer hall and the actual mausoleum.

Lastly, make sure to stop by Shinkyo Bridge, considered to be one of Japan's three finest bridges. If you're heading to the shrines and temples of Nikko from Nikko Station, you'll pass right by it. It's hard to miss.

Hakone: The Mountain Hot Springs Town

If you want a break from the big city, or you just want to add a bit of a getaway to your trip, you should definitely add a day trip to Hakone to your itinerary. It's famous for its *onsen* (Japanese hot springs), as well as its great views. Here, you can sit in a nice hot spring and enjoy views of Lake Ashinoko, and maybe even Mount Fuji.

Some of the top *onsen*-only destinations in Hakone include the following:

>> Tenzan

>> Hakone Yuryo

>> Yunosato Okada

>> Hakone Ginyu

However, many *onsen* are part of larger resorts. Some of the top *onsen* resorts include the following:

>> Kappa Tengoku

>> Hotel Green Plaza Hakone

>> Hakone Kamon

>> Ashinoko Hanaori

>> KAI Sengokuhara

If you really want a unique *onsen* experience, I recommend checking out Hakone Kowakien Yunessun. Although it does offer traditional hot spring baths, it also has somewhat of a waterpark attraction as well. The waterpark section has all sorts of unique *onsen*, such as wine-filled *onsen*, green tea *onsen*, and coffee *onsen*. However, unlike other traditional *onsen*, in the waterpark section of Yunessun, bathing suits are required (although they do offer a traditional *onsen* outside the waterpark section).

If you're in the mood for a scenic walk, you can stop by the Hakone Botanical Garden of Wetlands, Gora Park, the Hakone Detached Palace, and even Choanji Temple. Both the Hakone Botanical Garden of Wetlands and Gora Park offer trails through beautiful gardens. Gora Park has a western theme to its garden, while the botanical garden focuses on preserving marsh and alpine plants native to Japan. The Hakone Detached Palace actually served as the summer palace for the Imperial Family before being opened up to the public and offers great views of the lake and, on clear days, Mount Fuji. Last but not least, Choanji Temple is a small temple with a handful of walking trails and is famous for the couple hundred statues of *rakan* (disciples of Buddha) scattered around the temple grounds.

Kamakura: The Seaside Capital of Old Japan

Many places make for great side trips from Tokyo, but few are quite as full of history as Kamakura, the former capital of Medieval Japan. It's a great place for those who have an interest in Japanese history or who want to see more shrines and temples.

One of the most popular attractions in Japan is Kotokuin, which is known for its large Buddha statue set in the middle of the area. I still remember rounding the corner to be greeted by the statue and immediately stopping and thinking "Wow, that's a big Buddha." At 11.4 meters (37 feet), it's the second-tallest bronze Buddha statue in Japan.

There are numerous temples and shrines in Kamakura worth visiting, but here are some of the best:

>> **Tsurugaoka Hachimangu Shrine:** The approach to this shrine begins along the waterfront in the city center and takes you past several large *torii gates* (traditional Japanese gates often found at the entrances of shrines) before dropping you off at the main hall. Inside the main hall, you'll find the traditional offering box, as well as a small museum, which displays several treasures such as swords, masks, and other items of value.

>> **Kenchoji:** This temple is considered the first of Kamakura's five great Zen temples and is also the oldest Zen temple in Kamakura. Behind the main hall is a beautiful garden designed by Zen master Muso Kokushi. If you make your way toward the top of the temple grounds, you'll find an observation deck with great views of the main temple complex below.

- **Zeniarai Benten Shrine:** This shrine is tucked away up in a mountain, making it a bit of a hike to get to, but the journey is a really cool experience in itself. After you arrive, you actually have to walk through a small tunnel area to get to the shrine.

- **Engakuji:** Like Zeniarai Benten Shrine, part of the fun of visiting this temple is the journey. As you make your way there, you'll take a scenic walk past small ponds with traditional Japanese houses in the back tucked away behind some trees. The temple itself is considered the second of Kamakura's five great Zen temples and contains a handful of national treasures. Here you can also enjoy a cup of tea, *amazake* (sweet sake), or Japanese sweets.

Yokohama: Home to Chinatown

Ironically, Japan's second-largest city is located just half an hour away from the largest city!

You can do many different things in Yokohama, but probably one of the most popular is to stroll around Japan's largest Chinatown. You'll know you've arrived by the fancy, colorful gate that stands over each of the four entrances into the district. Here, you'll find countless restaurants and shops, all featuring Chinese-themed food and goods. Get a bite to eat and go window shopping. I was particularly fond of the street vendors who would draw dragons, clouds, suns, pandas, and other artwork in the shape of your name (actually spelling out the characters).

Also located in Yokohama are both the Ramen Museum and the Cup Noodle Museum. At the Ramen Museum, you can learn about the history of ramen and its introduction to Japan, but more excitingly, it features nine different ramen restaurants. Each restaurant features a different dish from a different part of Japan, allowing you to sort of tour the country's ramen scene without actually having to tour the whole country. Similar to the Ramen Museum, at the Cup Noodle Museum you can learn about the invention of instant noodles, as well as space ramen (for astronauts). However, most people are typically more excited by the many activities offered at the Cup Noodle Museum. These include the following:

- **>> My Cupnoodles Factory:** Create your own original cup noodle.
- **>> Cupnoodles Park:** Kids playground themed like a ramen factory.
- **>> Noodles Bazaar:** Restaurants selling noodle dishes from around the world.

If you want some great views, head over to the business district of Yokohama. Here, you'll find a small amusement park called Cosmo World. Inside the park, you'll find a Ferris wheel that provides some pretty good views of the city from the top. Alternatively, you can head over to Sky Garden, an observatory located on the 69th floor of Landmark Tower.

Pokémon lovers will want to head to Yokohama toward the end of the Olympics or right after to catch the dancing Pikachus. That's right: During this festival, parades of Pikachus can be found all over town. More information about the event can be found at https://tokyocheapo.com/events/dancing-pikachu-horde-yokohama.

Chiba: A Theme Park Adventure

Surprise! Narita International Airport, one of the most common airports for overseas visitors flying to Tokyo, isn't actually located in Tokyo. It's in Chiba! If you're flying into Narita International Airport, you'll already be in Chiba!

Aside from the airport, likely the most famous destination in Chiba is Tokyo Disney Resort, home to two Disney theme parks (Tokyo Disneyland and Tokyo DisneySea) plus countless hotels, shops, and more.

Another less popular but noteworthy attraction in Chiba is Mount Nokogiriyama, home to Nihonji Temple. The temple's main attraction is a 31-meter-tall (102-foot) stone statue of Buddha. As you make your way along the many walking paths, you'll also find 1,500 *rakan* (disciples of Buddha) statues.

Mount Fuji: One of Japan's Three Sacred Mountains

If you're lucky, you can get a good view of Mount Fuji from both Hakone and Yokohama, but if you really want to get a good view of the highest volcano in Japan, you'll want to get up close and personal.

If you're a big fan of hiking, you can actually climb all the way to the top of Mount Fuji. A total of four different trails lead to the top of the sacred mountain, but the most popular is Yoshida Trail. There are actually a total of ten stations that lead from the base of the mountain to the top, but because there are paved roads all the way up to the fifth station, most people actually begin their climb up the mountain from the fifth station. From the fifth station on the Yoshida Trail, it takes an average of five to seven hours to reach the top and approximately three to five hours to return. However, because the Yoshida Trail is famous for its view of the sunrise, many hikers stop at the seventh or eighth station or at one of the many mountain huts along the way to get a few hours of sleep before heading back out in the wee hours of the morning to make it to the peak in time for sunrise.

If hiking isn't your thing, there are still plenty of ways to get a great view of Mount Fuji. Around Mount Fuji are five different lakes, aptly named the Fuji Five Lakes:

>> **Lake Kawaguchiko** is the most accessible of the Fuji Five Lakes and is well developed. Here you'll find Fuji Q Highland, one of Japan's most popular amusement parks. In addition to the amusement park, attractions around Lake Kawaguchiko include Kawaguchiko Music Forest, which offers a small European-style garden and museum devoted to automatic musical instruments, and Mount Fuji Panoramic Ropeway, which leads to an observation point where Mount Fuji and Lake Kawaguchiko can be seen.

>> **Lake Saiko** isn't as popular a destination given that views of Mount Fuji are blocked by other nearby mountains. However, the exception to that is the very west side of the lake, where you can get a full view of the mountain. Around Lake Saiko you can try your hand at various Japanese

handicrafts and learn about the traditional lifestyle, explore some of the caves that were developed by previous eruptions of Mount Fuji, and check out the Iyashi no Sato observation deck.

>> **Lake Yamanakako** is the largest of the five lakes and is great for outdoors enthusiasts. Here you'll find many sports complexes that allow you to participate in boating, fishing, water skiing, camping, and more. It's also home to one of the few resorts that offer *onsen* with good views of Mount Fuji.

>> **Lake Shojiko** is the smallest of the lakes and also the least developed. However, there are a few hotels in the area, as well as hiking trails and other outdoor activities.

>> **Lake Motosuko** is most famous for being the image on the back of the ¥1,000 bill. Like many of the other lakes, it features a plethora of outdoor activities, such as camping, fishing, and more.

Sendai: Home to One of Japan's Most Powerful Lords

Sendai is a bit far for a day trip if you plan on driving or taking a bus — it would take you approximately four hours to get there — but if you go by bullet train, you can make it in a little under two hours.

In my opinion, Sendai is one of those hidden-gem types of destinations. You likely won't see it on any "top things to do in Japan" or "must do for first-time Japan visitors" lists, but it was one of my favorite destinations in Japan.

The city was founded around 1600 by Date Masamune, one of Japan's most powerful lords. Not long after, members of the Date clan ordered the construction of some of the city's most popular attractions including Osaki Hachimangu Shrine, Rinnoji Temple, and Zuihoden Mausoleum. Both Osaki Hachimangu Shrine and Zuihoden Mausoleum stand out for their intricate woodwork, contrasting red and black color, and ornate gold. Rinnoji Temple seems a little less impressive at first sight, but tucked away in the back is a beautiful walking garden.

Aside from Fushimi Inari in Kyoto (see Chapter 18), one of my favorite places in Japan is Risshaku-ji, which is actually just a bit outside Sendai. Its nickname, Yamadera (which is actually more widely known than its actual name), literally translates to "Mountain Temple." As I'm sure you can guess by the name, it's located on the side of a mountain. In order to reach the temple, you have to climb a thousand steps, but the view at the top of the valley below and mountains in the distance is totally worth it.

Nagoya: The Manufacturing Giant

Like Sendai, Nagoya is a bit far for a day trip if you're going by car (it would take about four hours one way). However, if you go by bullet train, it only takes about two hours, which is much more doable. Alternatively, it makes for a great stopover city if you plan on exploring other parts of Japan, such as Osaka or Kyoto (see Chapter 18).

TIP

Nagoya is definitely more of an off-the-beaten path type of destination. If this is your first time visiting Japan and you're limited on time, I would prioritize other day trips in this chapter or even other destinations in Japan over Nagoya. The exception to that is if you're one of the people who prefers to avoid the touristy places and get a much more authentic feel.

One of the top places to visit in Nagoya is Nagoya Castle. This is one of the many castles in Japan that have been rebuilt, which basically means that, while the outside still looks like a traditional castle, the inside is more like a modern museum. The museum exhibits are cool, but I think the best part of visiting Nagoya Castle is the Honmaru Palace, which is one of the buildings located within the castle grounds. Inside, you'll find traditional *shoji* (paper sliding doors that are decorated with exquisite paintings).

Aside from the castle, one of Nagoya's other biggest selling points is that the Toyota Motor Corporation headquarters is right outside the city. Car lovers will be thrilled to not only take a tour of the plant, but also see some of the newest models and technology on display.

If you prefer trains to cars, you'll want to check out the SCMAGLEV and Railway Park. Here you can see not only historic trains such as locomotives, but also more modern trains. In particular it features some of the experimental bullet trains and SCMAGLEV superconducting magnetic levitation (SCMAGLEV) trains that set new world records for railway speeds.

Also in Nagoya is Osu Kannon Temple, a popular temple in the Nagoya area. Although the temple is cool to check out, I actually recommend spending more time at Osu Kannon-dori, which is also referred to as Osu Shopping Arcade or Osu Shopping Street. Here you can find all sorts of mom-and-pop-style restaurants and shops. Because it's not nearly as touristy as some of the other shopping districts in Japan, it's a bit hit-or-miss as to whether the staff will speak any English. However, if you can manage to have a conversation with some of them, you'll quickly find that it's a great place to get good deals. I was able to find a used kimono in great condition for a really good price.

If you plan on arriving in Japan before the start of the Olympics and you're interested in seeing a sumo tournament, you may want to squeeze in a trip to Nagoya at the beginning of your itinerary. The July Grand Tournament will be held in Nagoya at the Aichi Prefectural Gymnasium (also known as the Dolphins Arena) from early to mid-July. More information about the tournament can be found on the Nihon Sumo Kyokai website at www.sumo.or.jp/ EnTicket/year_schedule.

Chapter **18**
Visiting Other Places in Japan

D ue to time and budget restrictions, you may only be able to go to Japan for the Olympics, and that's totally fine. However, if you have the bandwidth to do so, I definitely recommend extending your trip, if even only a little bit. There are so many other amazing places in Japan (see Figure 18-1). You've already made the trip — it would be sad not to be able to see at least a few of them.

FIGURE 18-1: A map of other places in Japan to visit.

Hiroshima: A City Reborn

Hiroshima is one of those places that tends to get left off many Japan itineraries, especially if it's a person's first time to Japan. Although it may not have some of the great shrines or culturally unique activities like Kyoto or Tokyo, it is rich in history.

THE ROLE OF THE ATOMIC BOMB IN WORLD WAR II

Near the end of World War II, an ultimatum, known as the Potsdam Declaration, called for the surrender of Japan and promised "prompt and utter destruction" if Japan did not surrender. A week and a half later, the United States dropped an atomic bomb on Hiroshima. It detonated about 1,900 feet above the city, leaving a 1-mile radius of total destruction and a 4-mile radius of fires. An estimated 90,000 to 140,000 people were killed as a result.

If you plan to visit Hiroshima, or even if you don't have time to add the city to your trip, well worth your time is reading *Hiroshima* by John Hersey (originally published in *The New Yorker* in 1946). You can read it for free on the website of *The New Yorker* at www.newyorker.com/magazine/1946/08/31/Hiroshima, or buy a copy in book form from your favorite bookstore.

If you do nothing else in Hiroshima, visit the Hiroshima Peace Memorial Park. As you explore this almost 30-acre park, you'll find several memorials and museums dedicated to the dropping of the atomic bomb. Honestly, few things have had as big of an effect on me as the memorials and museums located in this park. I'd dare say they hit me even harder than the 9/11 memorial in New York City.

At the northernmost end of the park, you'll come across the Atomic Bomb Dome, also called the Genbaku Dome or A-Bomb Dome, which is one of the only buildings to remain standing after the atomic bomb was dropped. Despite being only 490 feet from the detonation point, the unique architectural structure helped it survive the downward force of the bomb. It's also a UNESCO World Heritage Site, meaning that it has been identified by the United Nations Educational, Scientific, and Cultural Organization (UNESCO) as being an integral part of the area's cultural and natural heritage and having outstanding value to humanity.

Also in the Peace Memorial Park is the Children's Peace Monument, but in order to understand its significance, you first need to understand an important part of Japanese culture.

Legend states that a person who can fold a thousand origami cranes would be granted a wish. That's exactly what Sadako Sasaki tried to do. Sadako was only two at the time of the bombing, and was diagnosed with leukemia not long after, as were many other children who suffered from radiation exposure. She set out to make a thousand cranes in hopes of wishing for a world without nuclear weapons. Some accounts of the story state that she fell short of that goal before passing away; others state that she exceeded her goal. Today, the Children's Peace Memorial commemorates Sadako and all the other innocent, child victims of the bombing.

As you continue making your way south through the park, you'll reach the Memorial Cenotaph and Peace Flame. The Memorial Cenotaph is a saddle-shaped monument that covers a stone chest holding the names of all those who died due to the initial bombing or from exposure to radiation. On the other side of the pond from the Memorial Cenotaph is the Peace Flame, referred to as Heiwa no Tomoshibi in Japanese. It has been continuously burning since 1964 and will continue to burn until the end of nuclear weapons and warfare.

If you stand in front of the Memorial Cenotaph and face north, the arch of the Memorial Cenotaph perfectly frames both the Peace Flame and the Atomic Bomb Dome in the background.

Just a bit east of the Memorial Cenotaph and Peace Flame is the Hiroshima National Peace Memorial Hall. It was built to remember and mourn the victims, as well as express Japan's desire for lasting peace. The main exhibit is the Hall of Remembrance, which contains a panorama view of the city after the bomb went off. In the center of the Hall of Remembrance is a basin intended to offer water to the souls of the victims who died craving water that day and displays 8:15 a.m., the exact time the bomb went off. Outside the Hall of Remembrance is the Victims' Information Area, where you can see the names and photographs of many of the victims.

At the very south end of the park is the Hiroshima Peace Memorial Museum. Its exhibits not only describe what happened before and after the bomb, but also display personal artifacts and memorabilia from the event.

Some of the exhibits in this museum are a little grotesque, and that's done on purpose because they're meant to embody the grief, anger, and pain of real people. It's definitely not for the faint of heart, but I think it's a place that everybody should make an effort to visit. It's a tremendously eye-opening experience.

August 6, 2020 (a few days before the Olympic closing ceremony) will mark the 75th anniversary of the atomic bombing. In previous years, a ceremony has been held at Hiroshima Peace Memorial Park to remember and pray for the victims. If you can fit it into your itinerary, this would be the perfect day to visit Hiroshima.

Although most of the most popular attractions in Hiroshima focus around the atomic bomb, there are plenty of other things to do in Hiroshima not related to World War II. One of the most popular includes visiting the island of Miyajima.

Most people make the trip to Miyajima for Itsukushima Shrine, famous for its bright orange *torii gate* (the traditional Japanese gate often found at the entrances of shrines) that appears to float on water. However, this effect only happens when the tide is in. For that reason, I would typically recommend stopping by Itsukushima twice. When the tide is in, you can see the beautiful floating-on-water effect it's known for, but when the tide is out, you can actually walk all the way up to the gigantic torii gate. However, renovations on the torii gate began in June 2019, partially covering the gate with scaffolding. As of this writing, no completion date for the renovations has been set, but they're expected to take at least a year, so the gate may or may not be visible during the Olympics.

Kyoto: Stepping Back in Time to Old Japan

For those looking to experience traditional Japanese culture and almost step back in time to old Japan, you'll want Kyoto to be at the top of your bucket list.

Fun fact: During World War II, several other cities were considered to be targets for atomic bombs and Kyoto was actually favored for one of the very first attacks. However the U.S. Secretary of War at the time, Henry Stimson, persuaded President Truman that it should be removed due to its cultural importance. Thanks to Henry Stimson, countless shrines, temples, and other locations of cultural significance and historic value remain.

Personally, my absolute favorite shrine in all of Japan is Fushimi Inari, located in southern Kyoto. It's located on the side of Mount Inari and is famous for its thousands of torii gates. As you make your way along the trail to the top, you'll pass through many of the torii gates, many of which have been donated and have the names of the donor engraved on them. The shrine itself is dedicated to Inari, the Shinto god of rice. Because *kitsune* (foxes) are thought to be Inari's messengers, you'll see countless fox statues along the shrine grounds.

You'll also pass by several smaller shrines, as well as other establishments such as restaurants. I highly recommend stopping in one of the restaurants if you want to get a feel for traditional Japanese dining. Many of them have the old-style low tables and cushions on the floor instead of chairs. They also typically offer themed dishes, such as Kitsune Udon.

Another popular temple in Japan is Kinkakuji, which is completely covered in gold leaf. It sits overlooking a decent-size pond, and on a good day, you can see a perfect reflection of the temple in the water.

Rivaling Kinkakuji in popularity is Kiyomizu-dera (literally translates to "Pure Water Temple"). It's most famous for its wooden stage that serves as an observation deck, allowing visitors to get a nice view of the different types of trees that grow on the hillside, as well as the city in the distance.

TIP

At the bottom of the hill is also the Otawa Waterfall, which the temple is named after. It has three separate spouts, each said to provide a different fortune (longevity, success at school, and fortune in love) when drunk from. Visitors typically choose to pick one to drink from, because drinking from multiple spouts is considered greedy.

As mentioned earlier, Kyoto is full of other countless historic shrines and temples. Each has its own unique features that make it worth visiting. However, it's also possible to get sort of burned out with visiting shrines and temples, so I'd be a bit picky about which ones you decide to visit. Other notable shrines and temples in Kyoto include the following:

>> Ginkakuji

>> Nanzenji

- » Daigoji
- » Byodo-in
- » Shoren-in
- » Daitokuji
- » Honen-in
- » Anrakuji

One of the other things I recommend doing while in Kyoto is rent-ing *kimono,* the traditional clothing of Japan. Just don't do it on the same day you visit Fushimi Inari. The clothing can be a bit restrictive and the shoes hard to walk in, which makes climbing a mountain less than pleasant. I know — I learned the hard way.

Most (if not all) shops offer both men's and women's kimonos, as well as *yukata* (the lighter, summer version of kimono). They'll have several different colors and designs to choose from and will then help you put them on. Many shops also offer accessories or hair styling for an additional cost.

TIP

Make sure to use the restroom before having them help you into the kimono. It's not exactly easy (like, practically impossible) to use the restroom after you've donned a kimono.

WARNING

The other thing to keep in mind while wearing a kimono is to be careful when taking selfies with your phone. When wearing a kimono for normal occasions, the left side should be crossed on top of the right. Having the right crossed over the left is typically reserved for funerals. Depending on the phone and camera app, sometimes the mirror image gets captured, making it look like the kimono is crossed the wrong way.

One of the most popular attractions in Kyoto that isn't a shrine or temple is Arashiyama Bamboo Grove. Walking paths wind through the grove, allowing visitors to take a peaceful and quiet walk through the grove.

TIP

Arashiyama Bamboo Grove is great to visit anytime during the day, but if you want a truly tranquil experience, I recommend heading there first thing in the morning, because it can get pretty crowded during the day, especially on the weekend.

Instead of taking the bus to Arashiyama Bamboo Grove (because that is the normal mode of transit in Kyoto), I recommend check-ing out the Sagano Scenic Railway (also referred to as the Sagano

Romantic Train or Sagano Torokko). Unlike traditional trains, it's completely open on the sides (save for some railings), giving you an unobstructed view of Kyoto's natural beauty.

If you're a fan of Samurai, I recommend checking out Samurai Kembu Theater. Here, visitors get to learn about *Kembu*, the traditional sword art practiced by the ancient samurai of Japan. Depending on what kind of package you purchase, you can watch performances by masters of Kembu, and then even try it out for yourself!

Gion Matsuri, held at Yasaka Shrine in Kyoto, is the most famous festival in Japan. Lucky for you, it's held the entire month of July, which means you may get the opportunity to experience this amazing event if you decided to visit Japan before or during the first week of the Olympics.

Osaka: The Place for Modern Architecture and Nightlife

Just an hour's train ride from Kyoto is Osaka, Japan's second-largest metropolitan area.

One of the most popular attractions in Osaka is Osaka Castle. It was the first castle I ever visited in Japan, and I remember being amazed by the height of the stone walls that surrounded the castle (although at 5'0", everything seems tall to me). The moat that surrounds the castle looks more like it could be a beautiful river. Like the Nagoya Castle (see Chapter 17), it has been reconstructed, meaning the outside still looks like a traditional castle, but the inside is more like a modern museum. At the very top, you'll find an observatory that provides decent views of the city below.

The Floating Garden Observatory at Umeda Sky Building was one of my favorite observatories in Japan. At 170 meters (557 feet), it's definitely not the highest observatory in Japan. However, it is one of the only observatories that's open, allowing you to get a beautiful view of the city without any glass (don't worry, it still has railings so you can't fall off).

To the average person, not having to look through glass may not seem like a big deal, but to others (especially photographers), glass can be obstructive to getting a truly good view of the city, especially if other lights in the area cause a reflection on the glass. For a sight that will truly take your breath away, go at night so you can see the city all lit up.

Another popular attraction is Universal Studios Japan. Like many other theme parks, it offers an abundance of rides, places to eat, and shops. This particular Universal Studios park has eight different sections:

» Hollywood

» New York

» San Francisco

» Jurassic Park

» Waterworld

» Amity Village

» Universal Wonderland

» Wizarding World of Harry Potter

Kids (and even adults) will likely enjoy the LEGOLAND Discovery Center Osaka. It offers not only a factory tour and hands-on building activities, but also a few rides. And of course, there is a shop where you can buy as many LEGOs as your heart desires.

Also, don't forget to visit Dotonbori, Osaka's famous shopping street. It consists mostly of food shops, but it also has game centers, karaoke, clothing stores, and general markets. It's also where you'll find the Glico Man, a 33-meter (108-foot) sign depicting an athlete on a blue track. It's an ad for the local confectionery manufacturer, Ezaki Glico. Ever heard of Pocky (commonly found in the Asian section of many U.S. supermarkets)? Yeah, Ezaki Glico makes those. The Glico Man sign has become somewhat iconic in Osaka, and you'll often see tourists stopping to imitate the pose for a picture.

Nara: Japan's First Permanent Capital

One of the best things about the Kansai region in Japan is how much there is to do and see in such close proximity. Nara, a smaller but popular city, makes for a fantastic day trip from either Kyoto or Osaka.

If you forget for a second that Nara is second only to Kyoto when it comes to rich cultural sites in Japan, you'll find that Nara is also quite famous for its deer. Within Nara Park, you'll find countless deer that are completely unafraid of humans. You can literally walk right up to them, and they won't even flinch. For the most part, they'll either ignore you or come looking for food.

The deer are also sometimes referred to as the "bowing deer of Nara," because they'll often bow in expectation of receiving a treat as a reward. If you visit Nara Park, you can try purchasing some of the deer snacks (or "deer crackers") from nearby shops to see if you can get the deer to bow for you.

WARNING

For the most part, the deer are friendly, well natured, and non-aggressive, but never forget that they're wild animals. It's not uncommon for the deer to try to get your attention, especially if they think you have food. I watched one of the deer tug a visitor pamphlet right out of a tourist's hands (despite the person's best efforts to hold onto it) because the deer thought she had food. I've seen other deer somewhat gently tap their heads on people's legs or nip on people's clothing for food as well.

Probably the most famous attraction in Nara is Todaiji. Not only is it a UNESCO World Heritage Site, but it also houses Japan's largest bronze Buddha statue.

Todaiji is the main attraction within Nara Park, but there are several other smaller shrines and temples within and just outside the park that you can explore, including the following:

>> Nigatsuo-do and Sangatsu-do

>> Tamukeyama Hachimangu

>> Kasuga Taisha

>> Himuro Shrine

>> Kofukuji Temple

Himeji: Home to the White Heron Castle

For those who love Japanese tradition and history, no trip to Japan would be complete without a stop in Himeji, the home of one of Japan's most famous castles. Plus, due to its convenient location along the Sanyo Shinkansen (bullet train), it makes for another great day trip from Kyoto or Osaka or a stop along the way to Hiroshima.

Himeji Castle is often called Japan's most spectacular castle. It's also nicknamed the White Heron Castle due to its white appearance and overall layout. It's not only a national treasure but also a UNESCO World Heritage Site.

REMEMBER

Throughout this book, I mention other castles located around Japan. However, every other castle I've mentioned so far (and even in later chapters) are reconstructions of the original castle. This means that, although the outside of the castle looks the same as it originally did, the insides have been remodeled to be more like modern museums.

Himeji Castle is *not* a reconstruction. It was never destroyed by war or fire, making it one of the few remaining original castles in Japan. Sure, it has museum-like exhibits inside, but the interior still has the feel of a castle.

The side pillars (other parts of the castle) also give spectacular views of the main *keep* (fortified tower) and look just as spectacular on the inside, so make sure to allot enough time to explore the entire castle, not just the main keep.

Just a short walk from Himeji Castle is Kokoen Garden. Full of ponds, bridges, stone paths, and traditional Japanese buildings, you'll find that the beauty of the garden matches the beauty of the nearby castle.

Kokoen Garden actually consists of nine different gardens, separated by walls. It's a great place to just roam and follow whatever path you happen to come across, which is also a great way to get lost. I found that out the hard way. However, most people probably won't mind getting lost in such a beautiful place.

Okayama: Home to One of Japan's Best Gardens

Not only is Okayama the capital of Okayama Prefecture, but it's one of those "hidden gem" cities. It's not nearly as crowded with tourists as Tokyo or Kyoto, but it definitely has its claim to fame with iconic landmarks such as Crow Castle and one of the three great gardens in Japan.

If you've ever read the popular Japanese fairy tale Momotaro ("Peach Boy"), you'll be familiar with Okayama Castle. Due to its black color, it's often referred to as Crow Castle. Although the museum-like exhibits within the castle are cool, one of its unique features is a pottery studio where visitors can learn how to make *Bizen-yaki*, a type of pottery local to Okayama Prefecture.

Across from Okayama Castle is Korakuen Garden, ranked as one of Japan's three best landscape gardens. Like many Japanese landscape gardens, it features various ponds, bridges, and walking paths. It also has large open lawns, as well as dense forests. From certain spots in the garden, you can also see Okayama Castle peeking out from behind the trees, creating a nice backdrop for photos.

6

The Part of Tens

IN THIS PART . . .

Make sure you see all the top sights in Tokyo.

Learn which sports are the most exciting to watch.

Chapter **19**

Top Ten Things to Do in Tokyo

E very destination has "must-do" activities and attractions. You know, the ones that friends and family back home will be like, "You mean to tell me you went to Tokyo and didn't do *x*?" If you're trying to avoid that reaction, this chapter is for you.

Tsukiji Outer Market and Toyosu Market

The original Tsukuji Fish Market consisted of two different parts: the inner market (a wholesale market) and the outer market. However, in October 2018, the inner market was moved to Toyosu and reopened as the Toyosu Market.

The inner market, now Toyosu Market, is the world's largest fish market. It's such a popular spectacle that there are actually dedicated routes and observation windows specifically created for visitors to watch the auctions for tuna and other seafood and produce. If you would rather be up close and personal, you can apply for a lottery (http://pia.jp/piajp/v/toyosushijou19) where winners can view the auction from a much closer location. However, auctions typically take place between 5:30 a.m. and 6:30 a.m., meaning you'll need to wake up super early (or, you know, go to bed super late) if you want to catch the action.

Not all travel websites and guidebooks have been updated since the move of the fish market. Do not go to the Tsukuji Market if you're looking for the live auctions.

The Tsukuji Outer Market, the original outer market from the Tsukuji Fish Market, is still open and lively. It consists of many shops and businesses, which are typically open from 5 a.m. to about noon or a little later.

TIP

Because most shops get their food directly from the Toyosu Market, it's one of the best places in Tokyo to get fresh seafood.

Shinjuku Gyoen

Given that Tokyo is a large metropolis, you may be surprised to learn that there are actually a significant number of parks and gardens located within Tokyo. It's like Central Park in New York City, except that there's more than one Central Park.

Shinjuku Gyoen easily topped my list of best parks and gardens in Tokyo. From the 1600s to the mid-1800s, it was actually the home of a feudal lord before being transferred to the Imperial Family and eventually opened as a public park. It costs a few yen to enter, but it's well worth the money.

When you enter the park, it may seem like any other park at first, with just a dirt path leading you through some trees. However, after you make it into the core of the garden, you discover that it has so much more to offer than just a nice stroll. Inside, you'll find not only a traditional Japanese landscape garden, but also a formal French garden and English landscape garden as well.

If you have an hour or two between Olympic events, or just some free time to explore, make sure you take a stroll through the gardens, across the various Japanese-style bridges, around the traditional tea house, and through the conservatory. It's a great way to get away from the hustle and bustle of the city!

Meiji Jingu

Meiji Jingu, or Meiji Shrine, is another great way to get away from the hustle and bustle of the city, but in a very different way. The shrine is located in the middle of a densely populated forest and dedicated to the spirits of the late Emperor Meiji and Empress Shoken. During his rule, referred to as the Meiji Period, Japan went through great reform, including the breakdown of social classes, improvements in communication and transportation, as well as changes in the education and currency systems.

There are several different entrances to the grounds, making it easily accessible from both Harajuku Station and Yoyogi Station. From either of these entrances, it's about a ten-minute walk to the main shrine buildings.

Here, you can partake of typical practices performed at Shinto shrines:

TIP

>> **Purify yourself.** Most shrines will have a purification fountain near the entrance as a way to cleanse yourself before approaching the gods. Use the ladle to wash your left hand and then your right. Some visitors use the ladle to pour water into their hands for rinsing out their mouths.

>> **Make an offering and pray.** In the main hall, there will be an offering box where you can make an offering to the gods. Many choose to offer ¥5 because the Japanese phrase for ¥5 is 五円 (pronounced "go-en"), which is similar to ご縁 (also pronounced "go-en" and typically translated as "luck" or "destiny" or even "it was meant to be"). Gently drop your offering in the box, ring the bell (if there is one), and then bow twice, clap twice, and bow once more. Then make your silent prayer.

>> **Buy a charm or amulet.** Charms sold at Shinto shrines, referred to as *omamori,* are said to provide various forms of luck and protection. For example, there are omamori for happiness, education, good health, romance, and more. I bought one for safe travel and attached it to the backpack I always take with me when traveling.

Hachiko Statue

If you stumble across this statue near Shibuya Station by accident, you may think it's just a statue of some random dog. However, the story behind it is quite incredible.

There are a couple of different versions of the legend, but the main story is that Hachiko, an Akita dog, would go to Shibuya Station every day to meet his master on his way home from work. Even after his master passed away, Hachiko would continue to go to Shibuya Station to wait for his master every day until his own death nearly ten years later.

TIP

If you have some time during the flight to Japan (trust me, you will, it's a long flight) I recommend watching the movie *Hachi: A Dog's Tale,* which is a remake of the original *Hachiko Monogatari* movie that tells the full story of Japan's most faithful dog.

Shibuya Crossing

Right next to the Hachiko Statue is the Shibuya Crossing, also referred to as the Shibuya Scramble. It's rumored to be the busiest intersection, not just in Japan, but in the whole world. During peak rush hour, there can be upwards of 3,000 people crossing at one time. Nothing says "Welcome to the largest metropolitan area in the world!" more than being one of the thousands of people crossing the intersection at once.

TIP

After you've had your fill of the scramble, head up to one of the top floors in the nearby buildings to get a bird's-eye view of the scramble.

Senso-ji

Senso-ji, also known as Asakusa Kannon temple, is Tokyo's oldest temple. At the entrance of the temple grounds, you'll find Kaminarimon, or "Thunder Gate." As if the big red gate weren't prominent enough, a gigantic paper lantern with the Japanese characters for *Kaminarimon* written on it hangs in the center. Beyond Kaminarimon, you'll find Hozomon, the "Treasure House Gate," which houses much of the temple's treasures on the second floor. After you pass the two entrance gates, you'll find yourself in front of the main hall.

WARNING

Unlike Meiji Jingu, which was a Shinto shrine, Senso-ji is a Buddhist temple, which means the rituals are a bit different. Try the following:

>> **Purify yourself.** Temples often have purification fountains similar to shrines, but they also often have incense. The smoke is believed to have healing powers. For example, if you have a sprained wrist, you may use your good hand to wave the smoke toward your injured wrist.

>> **Make an offering and pray.** The procedure for praying at temples is similar to shrines. However, instead of bowing twice, clapping twice, and bowing once more, you simply bow once, say your silent prayer, and then bow once more.

Just outside the temple, you find Nakamise-dori, an entire street full of souvenir shops and food stalls. This street probably has the widest variety of souvenirs, but due to its popularity, it's also a bit more expensive than usual. If you're looking for simpler and cheaper souvenirs, I recommend heading over to Don Quijote (see the "Don Quijote" section, later in this chapter).

Tokyo Skytree

With a height of 634 meters (693 yards), Tokyo Skytree is the tallest tower and second-tallest freestanding structure in the world. It's almost the length of six football fields!

Its great height makes it one of the best places in Tokyo to get a view of the city. It actually has two different observation decks:

>> **Tembo Deck:** The Tembo Deck is approximately 350 meters (383 yards) up and has not only great views of the city, but also a souvenir shop, restaurant, and some glass panels on the ground that allow you to see all the way down to the base of the tower.

>> **Tembo Gallery:** The Tembo Gallery is 450 meters (492 yards) up and is more of a conventional observation deck. It's also on the list of top-ten highest observation decks in the world.

TIP

Personally, I recommend going just before sunset and then hanging around until evening. This way, you can see the city during the day, but also when it's completely lit up at night.

Takeshita-Dori

If you want to see some crazy Tokyo street fashion, this is the place to be. Located just in front of Harajuku Station, this street is chock-full of fashion-forward shops and restaurants.

If you stop by on a weekend, you'll likely see all sorts of young adults dressed in everything from neon-colored outfits to full punk-goth clothing. If nothing else, it's a great place to people-watch, as well as pick up some tasty sweets and candy.

If you're not a fan of crowds (and if you are, you chose the wrong city to visit), I recommend stopping by during the day on a weekday. The narrow street will be much less crowded, allowing you to explore the shops and enjoy the crêpes and other desserts with much less stress.

Purikura

Purikura is actually a shortened version of the Japanese phrase *Purinto Kurabu,* or "Print Club." To the unsuspecting passerby, it may seem like a typical photo booth you may see at your local mall. However, these photo booths have some fancy upgrades (think: Snapchat filters meets photo booth). When you enter the photo booth, you'll be able to take four to six photos. When you're done, you can go around to the other side of the photo booth where you can apply filters, make edits, and add stamps and stickers. In general, they tend to be a bit on the girly side, but I've seen some guys take some really cool photos, too!

You'll typically find purikura in arcades and game centers. Round1 Entertainment in the Ikebukuro district of Tokyo is a good place to start. The SEGA game centers in Ikebukuro and Akihabara, as well as the Adores arcades in Shinjuku, Shibuya, Ueno, Ikebukuro, and Akihabara are also great places for finding a variety of purikura.

Don Quijote

Don Quijote, sometimes shortened to Donki, is one of the largest discount stores in Japan. Many times these stores are so packed full of goods, it's practically impossible to look at everything! However, this also means it's one of the best places to pick up those random little things you forgot at home.

So, why did a discount store make it onto the list (albeit the bottom of the list) of the top ten things to do in Tokyo? It's a great place to find those unique, only-in-Japan types of items that make for great souvenirs. Here you can find USB sticks that look like popular Japanese snacks and *matcha* (green tea) flavored snacks (the Kit-Kats are especially popular). They also typically have other common souvenirs such as keychains, hats, chopsticks, and *yukata* (traditional Japanese summer clothing) for reasonable prices. Some even have hanko vending machines, where you can get a personalized *hanko* (Japanese seal) with your name on it.

Chapter **20**
Top Ten Olympic Events to Watch

I t's an undeniable truth: Some sports are just more popular or interesting to watch than others. That's not to say that they're better or more worthy than others. Personally, I'm a big fan of archery, but who else besides me actually watches the archery events? Not many. Certain sports have managed to capture the attention of viewers for multiple reasons, whether it's because the rules are simple and the competitions are relatable, or because the athletes do things we never even imagined possible. Find out what will be some of the top events to watch at the Tokyo 2020 Olympics.

Opening and Closing Ceremonies

The opening and closing ceremonies are some of the largest celebrations held in the whole world. Unfortunately, they're traditionally some of the hardest events to get tickets for, but they're definitely worth it if you can manage to get them.

Part of what makes the opening and closing ceremonies so spectacular is not just the lights and performances, but also the meaning behind the demonstrations. The Games Vision consists of three core concepts: "striving for your personal best," "accepting one another," and "passing on a legacy for the future."

The Tokyo 2020 Olympic Ceremonies specifically will focus on eight different concepts:

>> Peace

>> Coexistence

>> Reconstruction

>> Future

>> Japan and Tokyo

>> Athletes

>> Involvement

>> Excitement

It will be exciting to see exactly how Japan incorporates these points into the ceremonies. If nothing else, it will be a spectacular display, for sure!

Track and Field

Track and field is one of those Olympic sports that is loved for both its simplicity and its competitiveness. For most track events, the object is simple: to reach the finish line before the other racers. It's something we can relate to. Racing is something that all of us have likely done at least once in our lives, whether it was in school or just a friendly competition among friends.

Yet, despite its simplicity, it keeps everyone on the edge of their seats. Why? Because races are often won by less than a sliver. In the 2016 Summer Olympics, Usain Bolt beat Justin Gatlin for the gold medal in the 100-meter race by eight-hundredths of a second. In turn, Gatlin only beat Andre De Grasse by two-hundredths of a second.

Other track events combine both speed and endurance, challenging the athletes' ability to pace themselves while still trying to stay ahead of the other racers, making them as much mental as physical games.

The field events also display great athleticism and give spectators the opportunity to observe great accomplishments that you don't see every day. When was the last time you watched somebody throw a javelin 98 meters (107 yards)?

Gymnastics

Unlike other sports like track and field or swimming, where viewers can truly relate to the sport, gymnastics is one of those sports that make the athletes seem more like magicians. Sure, I can kick a soccer ball from one field to the other — not very well, but I can physically do it. Ask me to do a triple flip off a balance beam? Yeah, not in a million years. At the end of the day, it's just really cool to see gymnasts perform stunts that are seemingly impossible.

The sport has also increased in difficulty, making it even more of a spectacle. In 2006, the introduction of the Code of Points, a new rulebook defining the scoring system for gymnastics, encouraged athletes to make routines more and more difficult instead of playing it safe in order to focus on technique execution.

One of the other unique aspects of gymnastics is that it's one of the few Olympic sports that requires a great deal of creativity along with athleticism. Many of the routines are as much of a dance performance as they are skilled execution of techniques. On top of that, every single movement has to be executed absolutely perfectly.

Simone Biles, the most decorated gymnast in history, will also likely be returning to the stage for the Tokyo 2020 Olympics and is almost guaranteed to put on a good show.

Swimming

The Tokyo 2020 Olympics will be the first Summer Olympics since 2000 where Michael Phelps, the most decorated Olympian of all time, won't be competing. However, that hasn't made the sport of swimming any less interesting.

It's a sport of great diversity, with a total of four different types of techniques, or *strokes*, that are completed across all sorts of varying distances.

Like many sports, the sport of swimming is constantly evolving, but athletes are also constantly innovating. This innovation in techniques has allowed seven new world records to be set in swimming between the 2012 and 2016 Olympics. What world records do you think will be set in this Summer Olympics?

Basketball

Part of what makes basketball so interesting to watch is the fact that you typically never have to wait too long for a point to be scored. This means that there is always something exciting going on.

As if the continuous scoring weren't enough excitement, the performance of the players adds even *more*. There are dunks, alley-oops, and all sorts of other exciting plays to capture your attention.

Plus, some of the most intense games in basketball come down to the very last few seconds of the game to determine who the winner will be.

Part of what else makes Olympic basketball, in particular, so exciting is that players must play for their home countries. This means that some international players who traditionally play in the NBA in the United States may be returning home to play for their respective countries and facing off against the United States.

Soccer

Soccer is one of the most popular sports around the world, and it has seen countless victorious teams over the years. Brazil took home the gold in 2016, and other countries such as Mexico and Argentina have taken home the gold in recent Summer Olympic Games. Who do you think will take home the gold in 2020?

Unlike other sports such as basketball, soccer is a very low-scoring game, with some games going into overtime with a score of 0-0. However, that's always what contributes to some of the excitement. When an athlete kicks at the goal, will it go in? Will they score that coveted point that could ultimately make the difference in who wins the game?

Even between goals, athletes put on quite a show. From their fancy footwork to juking defenders to outsmarting the goalie, there is always something interesting going on.

Volleyball

Many sports require good teamwork and communication, but volleyball seems to require more than most. Teammates have to work together perfectly in order to not only retrieve a ball hit to their side, but also set up another player to spike the ball back to the opponent's side of the court. If you look really closely, you may even see players holding up fingers behind their backs when communicating to other team members.

Part of what makes the sport so exciting to watch is not only the speed at which players can spike the ball over the net, but also the heights they can reach. Some players are more than 6'5" tall and can reach heights of over 11 feet when attempting to spike or block the ball.

Judo

Given that judo originated in Japan, this sport holds a special place in the hearts of many Japanese, making it one of the more popular sports for the 2020 Summer Olympics.

Like many martial art sports, it's full of bursts of actions. For much of the match, athletes will do feints and teases, sort of feeling their opponents out, waiting for them to make mistakes that will give them an opening. When an athlete does decide to make her move, it's a sudden rush as both try to defend and gain the upper hand, ultimately allowing her to pin her opponent.

Rugby

Although American football is not an Olympic sport, Americans may find rugby just as entertaining. It has significant differences, but it still carries much of the same excitement.

Even though only the ball carrier can be tackled in rugby, there is still quite a bit of tackling going on. A study published in 2012 revealed that a total of 31,655 tackles were recorded across 48 professional rugby league matches. That's an average of 659 tackles per game!

What makes it even more amazing is that rugby can be played with just a mouthguard. Unlike in American football where players wear hard, heavy padding, in rugby only light padding on the head and shoulders is allowed.

Sport Climbing

Sport climbing is one of the new sports making its debut in the 2020 Olympics, and it's worth watching for the same reason as gymnastics. Sure, in sport climbing you don't have athletes performing beautiful routines to fancy music, but you'll see them do some absolutely incredible things.

Not convinced? Go to your favorite video-streaming website (such as YouTube) and search for "speed climbing." With the way these athletes can scale an almost 50-foot wall in six to seven seconds, I wouldn't be surprised if one of them were secretly Spider-Man.

Index

About the Author

Celeste Kiyoko Hall is the owner of Footsteps of a Dreamer (https://footstepsofadreamer.com), a travel website dedicated to helping readers plan their next trip. A frequent traveler herself, she has helped countless travelers plan their trips to Japan.

Her travel inspiration stemmed from a strong passion in her Japanese heritage. She has dedicated a significant portion of her life to helping others learn more about Japan and the culture. As a board member of the Midwestern Japan Student Associations and president of the Japanese Cultural Exchange Circle, she helped university students learn more about Japanese culture and customs. She continues that tradition by participating in online communities related to Japan travel and publishing Japan travel content on her website.

Dedication

To my mother, Joyce, and boyfriend, Zach, for their constant support in all my endeavors, and to my dad, Ron, who never got to see my dreams come true.

Author's Acknowledgments

I'll admit, the idea of writing a *For Dummies* book never crossed my mind until the opportunity landed in my lap (or really my inbox). Japan is a topic I'm intimately familiar with, but writing a book about it still ended up being significantly harder than I had expected.

I dedicated this book to my mother and boyfriend because I never would have been able to write this book if it weren't for them. They believed in me even when I didn't believe in myself. As my mom would say, "I owe them one."

Unfortunately, my dad passed away back in 2012, but if it weren't for him, I don't think I would have ever developed an interest in Japan. I didn't get to tell him how amazing it was to study abroad in Japan, or that I got the opportunity to write this book, but I know he would be proud of me. I'll forever be grateful to him for his role in helping me become who I am today.

I'm also grateful to the Japanese Department and Office of Global Education at Kent State University and the International Office at Rikkyo University for continuously providing me with opportunities to learn more about Japanese language and culture, as well as allowing me to extensively travel the country. A special shout-out to Eriko-sensei and Chris-sensei who always encouraged me in my studies and were instrumental in providing me with those opportunities.

Last, but definitely not least, I'd like to thank everyone involved in the publication of this book, because it never would have come to fruition without them. Thanks to John Wiley & Sons, especially Audrey Lee, editorial intern, and Ashley Coffey, acquisitions editor, for considering me for this opportunity, and Elizabeth Kuball, my amazing editor. Also, thanks to technical reviewer Anne Sutherland-Smith, who reviewed the bulk of the book, and Charles Andrews, who made sure my Japanese in Chapter 14 was correct.

Publisher's Acknowledgments

Acquisitions Editor: Ashley Coffey

Project Editor: Elizabeth Kuball

Copy Editor: Elizabeth Kuball

Technical Editors:
Anne Sutherland-Smith,
Charles Andrews

Production Editor:
Tamilmani Varadharaj

Cover Photos: © Sean Pavone/
Getty Images

Take dummies with you everywhere you go!

Whether you are excited about e-books, want more from the web, must have your mobile apps, or are swept up in social media, dummies makes everything easier.

Find us online!

dummies.com

Leverage the power

Dummies is the global leader in the reference category and one of the most trusted and highly regarded brands in the world. No longer just focused on books, customers now have access to the dummies content they need in the format they want. Together we'll craft a solution that engages your customers, stands out from the competition, and helps you meet your goals.

Advertising & Sponsorships

Connect with an engaged audience on a powerful multimedia site, and position your message alongside expert how-to content. Dummies.com is a one-stop shop for free, online information and know-how curated by a team of experts.

- Targeted ads
- Video
- Email Marketing
- Microsites
- Sweepstakes sponsorship

20 **MILLION**
PAGE VIEWS
EVERY SINGLE MONTH

15 MILLION **UNIQUE**
VISITORS PER MONTH

43%
OF ALL VISITORS
ACCESS THE SITE
VIA THEIR MOBILE DEVICES

700,000 NEWSLETTER SUBSCRIPTION
TO THE INBOXES OF
300,000 UNIQUE INDIVIDUALS EVERY WEEK

# of dummies

Custom Publishing

Reach a global audience in any language by creating a solution that will differentiate you from competitors, amplify your message, and encourage customers to make a buying decision.

- Apps
- eBooks
- Audio
- Books
- Video
- Webinars

Brand Licensing & Content

Leverage the strength of the world's most popular reference brand to reach new audiences and channels of distribution.

For more information, visit dummies.com/biz

PERSONAL ENRICHMENT

Staying Sharp	Facebook	Guitar	Investing	Beekeeping	Digital Photography
9781119187790	9781119179030	9781119293354	9781119293347	9781119310068	9781119235606
USA $26.00	USA $21.99	USA $24.99	USA $22.99	USA $22.99	USA $24.99
CAN $31.99	CAN $25.99	CAN $29.99	CAN $27.99	CAN $27.99	CAN $29.99
UK £19.99	UK £16.99	UK £17.99	UK £16.99	UK £16.99	UK £17.99

Meditation	Pregnancy	Samsung Galaxy S7	iPhone	Crocheting	Nutrition
9781119251163	9781119235491	9781119279952	9781119283133	9781119287117	9781119130246
USA $24.99	USA $26.99	USA $24.99	USA $24.99	USA $24.99	USA $22.99
CAN $29.99	CAN $31.99	CAN $29.99	CAN $29.99	CAN $29.99	CAN $27.99
UK £17.99	UK £19.99	UK £17.99	UK £17.99	UK £16.99	UK £16.99

PROFESSIONAL DEVELOPMENT

Windows 10	AutoCAD	Excel 2016	QuickBooks 2017	macOS Sierra	LinkedIn	Windows 10
9781119311041	9781119255796	9781119293439	9781119281467	9781119280651	9781119251132	9781119310563
USA $24.99	USA $39.99	USA $26.99	USA $26.99	USA $29.99	USA $24.99	USA $34.00
CAN $29.99	CAN $47.99	CAN $31.99	CAN $31.99	CAN $35.99	CAN $29.99	CAN $41.99
UK £17.99	UK £27.99	UK £19.99	UK £19.99	UK £21.99	UK £17.99	UK £24.99

SharePoint 2016	Fundamental Analysis	Networking	Office 2016	Office 365	Salesforce.com	Coding
9781119181705	9781119263593	9781119257769	9781119293477	9781119265313	9781119239314	9781119293323
USA $29.99	USA $26.99	USA $29.99	USA $26.99	USA $24.99	USA $29.99	USA $29.99
CAN $35.99	CAN $31.99	CAN $35.99	CAN $31.99	CAN $29.99	CAN $35.99	CAN $35.99
UK £21.99	UK £19.99	UK £21.99	UK £19.99	UK £17.99	UK £21.99	UK £21.99

dummies.com

dummies
A Wiley Brand